Except where otherwise indicated, Scripture
quotations are from the New Revised Standard
Version of the Bible: Anglicised Edition,
copyright © 1989, 1995 National Council of
the Churches of Christ in the United States of
America. Used by permission. All rights
reserved.

Other translations used: J. B. Phillips, 'The New
Testament in Modern English', 1962 edition by
HarperCollins.

All emphases supplied by the author.

The picture of James Hudson Taylor is used with
the permission of OMF international.

ISBN 978-1-78665-024-5

© 2017 The Stanborough Press Ltd
Published by The Stanborough Press Ltd,
Grantham, Lincolnshire, UK.

Designed by David Bell
Cover design by David Bell
Printed in Serbia

Being
Church
Missional, Accessible and Engaging

Adrian Peck

Contents

Acknowledgements

Writing a book is demanding, but I am very thankful that the task was made easier with the support, encouragement, advice and challenges provided by the following:

Dr Daniel Duda
Pastor Llewellyn Edwards
Pastor Gifford Rhamie
Dr Peter Roennfeldt
Pastor Aristotle Vontzalidis
Pastor David West

I would also like to thank my wife, Melody, for putting up with me spending hours at my computer!

A note from the Publisher
This book is based on the author's research into the steady growth of two non-Adventist congregations in the United Kingdom. Both started as humble church plants, but have bucked the all-too-common trend of sluggish growth or decline that has become the norm in this part of the world.

Although his observations are based largely on these two thriving congregations – Kingsgate Community Church in Peterborough, and Christchurch London – they highlight principles that are relevant to the work of Christian witness and mission everywhere. Those readers who live in countries where the church is in decline among people of European descent will find the author's ideas particularly useful. Hopefully it will give each reader something worthwhile to reflect on.

How to Use This Book

This book has been arranged into five sections covering different aspects of what it is to 'be Church'. The first section explores a biblical understanding of the Church in both its universal and local incarnations, particularly focusing on the concept of being God's dwelling place. An exploration of the Church's purpose follows, with a discussion on how this plays out in the way that a local congregation participates in God's mission. Sections three and four go on to consider how the biblically-based values of accessibility and engagement can help frame what such a church should be. The final section reflects on the manner in which a local church's context influences the way that church is, and, again, should be.

Each section consists of a number of parts, each concluding with a series of thought-provoking questions.

Whether working through the book on your own or in a group, the intention is not necessarily to provide solutions, but to encourage a different mode of thinking and being through a process of self-reflection. This is because it is not enough to read about what others are doing or how they think, but rather to apply what is discovered to our own specific situations, to the communities and individuals who reside within our sphere of influence. The thought questions are therefore designed to help initiate this process. The parts of each section vary in length, so, if working through this book as part of a small group, it may be appropriate to cover more than one section during a sitting.

Introduction

Sometimes it seems as if our church is like someone trying to lose weight. We all know people who think that in order to slim down you must try the latest, most trendy dieting regime. From the '5-and-2' diet to the 'zone' diet, on to the 'cookie' diet and the raw-food diet, there is always another to try. The latest plan, often with increasingly quirky and disturbing rules, is initially embraced with great enthusiasm. The answer to a new and slimmer you is believed to be tantalisingly close, just around the next corner! It's merely a case of finding the right method and the mirror will forever be your friend; the beach, your natural environment. Often there is an initial degree of success, but no diet seems to be entirely satisfactory or effective, and so hope is eventually supplanted by despair or transferred to the next dietary regime.

When it comes to encouraging growth in the Adventist Church in Western Europe, Britain in particular, it is much like with those diet plans. Anyone who has been a member for more than five minutes can probably reel off a list of solutions, programmes and initiatives that have been suggested to be the solution to our lack of growth. Glamorous, charismatic and articulate speakers have been flown in to 'run campaigns' or have had their presentations beamed across the country. The five-day plans to stop smoking, which were so in vogue in the '70s and '80s, are now supplemented or replaced by health expos. Messy churches have been set up, contemporary services or cafe churches established, community chaplaincy programmes commenced, and visitors' days instituted. Like a never-ending list of dieting regimes, the solution to church growth can seem, at times, to be just over the horizon, enticingly out of reach. But, despite some initial, and maybe qualified, success, none has proved to be fool-proof or long-lasting.

One thing to bear in mind here is that, on one level, losing weight is easy – simply eat less and wisely, and move more. However, the £1.8bn market for diet foods alone in the UK,[1] not counting the cost of weight-loss pills, books, DVDs and organisations such as Weightwatchers®, actually shows that losing weight is not quite such a stroll in the park. It is not straightforward, because the reasons why someone might put on weight and then fail to lose it are extremcly complex – affected by a range of sociological, genetic, psychological and environmental factors, among many others.

The answer to the problem comes down to more than just the food a person eats. It is also influenced by such things as personality, attitudes and DNA. It comes down to who we are and what makes us that way. Similarly, church growth has to do as much with people and who they are, as it does with what a given church or group of people are doing or not. As with a person trying to lose weight, the solution to the problem of non-growing churches might well be found at the very heart of who and what those churches are, their 'personality' and 'attitudes', their DNA and genetic structure.

Which evangelistic method is undertaken is, of course, important; and may well turn out to include either a messy church or a contemporary service, for example. However, if the fundamental structure and nature of the Church is not understood and lived out, then, no matter what is done to encourage church growth, we are setting ourselves up to struggle and ultimately fail. Trying to grow in ways that do not resonate with who we are is like the person who grows naturally to 5'10" and then tries, through the use of willpower, stretching and other techniques to break through the 6-foot barrier. If you are not 6 foot and have stopped growing, there is little you can reasonably do to gain those extra two inches . . . it's just not who you are meant to be.

The approach adopted in this book is to explore the issue of church growth by looking at what a church is, not primarily at what a church does. Now, of course, being church means doing something too; 'being' and 'doing' are not so easily compartmentalised. Therefore this is not, nor can it be, a book about church growth that is devoid of discussion about what to do. The intention is, however, to explore the relationship between who and what a church is and how this consequently influences what a church does. Therefore the basic thesis to be found in this book is that what we do to grow should flow from who we are as churches – our state of being, our nature.

The approach I have adopted emphasises the need to look at church growth from the perspective of the church – not just the individual. The individual approach looks to attain to the ideal of what the *Church Manual* calls 'every-member evangelism'. Such an approach may lead us to infer that the problem resides at the level of the individual, not the collective. This leads us to put measures in place that are designed to encourage the correct levels of personal spirituality and fervour among members. We also make every effort to ensure that individuals are trained to be effective witnesses. Now, it is indisputable that equipping and training members is of vital importance. However, a more complete picture, a picture that includes the perspective of what church is all about, locates those individuals in a living, breathing, spiritual community. Thus, the perspective is primarily that of the collective, rather than the individual.

Theories are fine, but experience, to paraphrase Stephen Hawking, breathes fire into them. To that end, research has been carried out into growing churches to help put meat on the bones, or, perhaps more appropriately for our Adventist context, soya beans on the plant. Before giving some background about the churches that were studied, there are a couple of 'housekeeping' issues to cover.

One of the major ways that churches are currently growing is through immigration. In very many ways this has been a blessing for the Adventist Church, both in the UK and in many other Western countries, as those arriving from other countries have brought life and vitality to diminishing congregations. But it is those churches that demonstrate that they are able to grow by reaching out to those who are indigenously or culturally British that is the primary focus

here. Growth through immigration is potentially unreliable in the medium-to-long term, as levels of immigration are subject to the vagaries of public opinion, the economic climate and government policy.

But of more concern than these factors is that the children and grandchildren of immigrants inevitably become acculturated and so adopt local customs, language and attitudes. This happens in spite of the influence of their parents and grandparents who come from countries that are seemingly more religious and spiritual than we are in the UK. Struggling to reach out to the 'British' of today will mean struggling to reach out to those who are becoming tomorrow's Brits – Westernised, secularised, postmodernised, or however you want to describe them. The research has looked, therefore, at churches that are principally British in terms of composition or have predominantly culturally British congregations. The objective is to look at churches that are succeeding where the Adventist Church in Britain and elsewhere (USA, Australia, etc) is struggling at best, and failing at worst, in the majority of cases.

A second element to consider is how the 'growth' part of church growth can be understood. Churches are spiritual enterprises and so growth is, at its heart, a spiritual matter. As God tells Samuel in 1 Samuel 16:7:

' ". . . for the LORD does not see as mortals see; they look on the outward appearance, but the LORD looks on the heart." '

Joel Osteen paraphrases this verse by writing, *'Only God can look at somebody's heart.'* This means that all of the ways of measuring church growth that look at external factors are, by comparison, limited. Verbal assent to doctrines and the public display of commitment and conversion bound up in the baptismal service, remain external views associated more with an institution than the spiritual enterprise that is Church. For if Church is about people relating to each other and to God; if it is about a people who are called out by God and living under His principles and values: then such things can only be understood organically and internally.

For the purposes of the research, attendance at a church's services was used as the basis for establishing whether any given church was in growth. Obviously, the above discussion about the internalised nature of Church has identified this as a restricted way of identifying growth – but it is a necessarily pragmatic one. The crucial aspect when selecting the churches for study was not only that they were growing numerically, but also that they were doing this by reaching out to those who are British – culturally or by birth. In this respect, the two churches described below satisfy these criteria by seemingly going against the trend of decline or stagnation seen among many British-based congregations.

Case Study 1:
Kingsgate Community Church, Peterborough

It is easy to feel overwhelmed when visiting Kingsgate Community Church in Peterborough, spread as it is over a sprawling 12.4 acres. Rather than the usual struggle to park, you drive into an extravagant 400-plus-space car park. The church building itself is a multimillion-pound facility that boasts a 1,600-seat auditorium and additional conferencing facilities. However, a glance at Kingsgate's backstory reveals much more humble beginnings. It started life as a small church plant in Dave and Karen Smith's front living

room with seven other people in 1988. From such modest beginnings, now, some 29 years later, Kingsgate sees just under 2,000 people attend the two morning services it offers on a Sunday. Initially, Kingsgate started off life as the Peterborough Community Church, but changed its name to Kingsgate as they found that they were attracting people from all over the region. However, not content to sit on their laurels, Kingsgate have also started running services and meetings in Cambridge, Spalding and Leicester.

Perhaps one of the few churches in Britain to even begin to qualify as a so-called megachurch, it is their continuing thirst for growth and reaching out to those who do not yet know Christ that is the most striking aspect of what they are about. Even though they might be regarded as verging on the uniquely successful, the attitudes and values embedded into their organisational culture can help inform any church.

Case Study 2:
Christchurch, London

Christchurch London had similarly small beginnings. It was started in 2004 by church planter David Stroud,[2] and within six months of the first meeting in April 2004, a congregation of 90 had been established.[3] At the time of writing, approximately 600 people attend over the two services it runs on a Sunday. Christchurch retains and values a high degree of flexibility and adaptability. As part of this approach, Christchurch hires venues rather than buying or leasing a building. This has allowed Christchurch to move into increasingly bigger and better facilities as the church has grown. Their current location is the Mermaid Theatre in Blackfriars – right in the heart of London.

Their concerns for having an impact on the communities in which they live and communicating the Gospel effectively are aspects that will help inform the discussion. Being led by Stroud, someone who has successfully planted several churches, means that the principles and values that drive his members, both organisationally and personally, can cast light in a practical way on the topic of this book.

[1]Figure for the UK for 2013. Source: Mintel.
[2]Stroud was also involved with planting King's Arms in Bedford – see: David Stroud, *Planting Churches – Changing Communities: A Hands-on Guide to Successful Church Planting* (Milton Keynes: Authentic, 2009).
[3]'ChristChurch London Explore' *http://christchurchlondon.org/aboutus* [accessed 21 July 2013].

SECTION 1

Being Church

I t is not so easy to extract a church from the building with which it is associated. As Frank Viola and George Barna suggest, *'Many contemporary Christians have a love affair with bricks and mortar.'*[1] One might doubt at first whether Adventists should also be included in this group, because, if the average Sabbath school class is asked to give a definition of 'church' they invariably – with one voice – will suggest it is the 'people' and definitely not the building in which those people are located. Often, the congregation is greeted with a hearty 'Hello, church!' that only makes sense if the speaker is addressing the congregation, and not the floors, walls and ceiling!

However, on those occasions when I have asked groups to sketch an image of 'church' on a piece of paper, roughly a third drew a group of people, a third a building, and the final

group drew both. This betrays a practical struggle we have to think about church as a group of people, as opposed to church as a building in which programmes and activities occur. Our language most often demonstrates this thinking, as church is what 'one goes to and attends'. Church is something that 'is or is not enjoyable'. Church 'lets us down, fails to meet our needs, feeds us, excites us and sometimes deflates us'. Church is frequently spoken about in the third person, as if it were something separate from us.

Yet, somewhere, perhaps at the back of our minds, we know this is nonsense, of course. If 'church' is a collective noun for people, when we are talking about 'our church', we are in reality talking about ourselves. If church is boring, that means you and I are boring. If church has let me down – the nature of church means that I have some responsibility for my own sense of disappointment.

Anyone who has ever sat for any time on a church board will know that a church building and its fixtures and fittings are among the most contentious of topics. From choosing the colour of a new carpet, via seating arrangements, through to just moving the location of the pulpit or other pieces of furniture . . . these are the agenda items that often raise the passions, entail hours of debate and demonstrate how much we care about the 'sanctuary', our church buildings and their layouts.

And so, it is easy to forget that one of the most radical things that Jesus did was move things away from being about a building to being about and focusing on people. Before Jesus, the centre of Israel's worship and religious life was the sanctuary; this was where God was to be found. But Jesus' coming changed all that, and this revolution is considered next.

Thought questions:

1. What is your mental image of 'church'?
2. Why is the concept of 'church' so readily associated with its building?
3. Even if a group doesn't have a church building, often their aim is to get one. Is it really possible to think of church as just being about people?

Being God's Dwelling Place: Part I

Where buildings are concerned, there are a number of texts in the Old Testament that refer to God dwelling among His people; but this is always with reference to the sanctuary found initially on the Sinai Peninsula, but intermittently and eventually in Jerusalem. An example of such a text is found in Exodus 29. This chapter is all about God establishing Aaron and his sons as priests, and the consecration of the newly constructed sanctuary itself. This process subsequently enables God to declare in verse 45, 'I will dwell among the Israelites, and I will be their God.'[12] It was the sanctuary and all that it entailed that meant that God was able to be understood to be living among His chosen people, Israel, in a special way.

Later, as the more permanent temple in Jerusalem was established and re-established, the focus was still on a particular building, but it was now of course in a fixed location. Hence, Ezra 7:15 refers to 'the God of Israel, whose dwelling is in Jerusalem', and similarly in Ezekiel 37:26-27 we find God declaring, 'I will bless them and multiply them, and will set my sanctuary among them for evermore. My dwelling place shall be with them; and I will be their God, and they shall be my people.' As Karl Barth suggested, in the Old Testament 'there is always a dwelling place of God which can be marked on the map'.³

 By the time we get to the period during and after the first advent, however, the situation has changed drastically. For now, it is not about God's dwelling place, but God's dwelling places. It is not about a physical location, with physical features, but about spiritual locations and spiritual buildings. This is a shift from thinking about God dwelling in a holy place to Him residing in holy people. This development, with great symbolic significance, was graphically and almost theatrically demonstrated through events that accompanied Jesus' death on the cross. As 'Jesus cried again with a loud voice and breathed his last', Matthew reports that at 'that moment the curtain of the temple was torn in two, from top to bottom. The earth shook, and the rocks were split.' Matthew 27:50, 51. As Ellen White reminds us, this seismic event showed 'that the great final sacrifice had been made, and that the system of sacrificial offerings was forever at an end'.⁴

Jesus had previously hinted at what was going on here with regard to the status of the temple, when He said, 'Destroy this temple, and in three days I will raise it up' (John 2:19). Just two days on from this very moment of supreme sacrifice, a new temple would be established; namely, 'the temple of [Jesus'] body' (John 2:21). No longer would it be possible to locate God's dwelling place on a map. Now, the focus would be on Jesus Himself, who after all was and is Immanuel, God with us – a mysterious and magnificent union of the human and the Divine.

Of course, it should not have been understood that God was to be confined to one specific place. Even when Solomon dedicated the first Jerusalem temple, he emphasised in his prayer that, where God is concerned,

'Even heaven and the highest heaven cannot contain you, much less this house that I have built!' 2 Kings 8:27. Stephen, in his remarkable speech found in Acts 7, feels moved to remind his listeners of this same fact when he quotes from Isaiah 66:1, 2, as he says, 'Heaven is my throne, and the earth is my footstool. What kind of house will you build for me, says the Lord, or what is the place of my rest? Did not my hand make all these things?' Acts 7:49, 50. Stephen felt he needed to remind listeners he characterised as 'stiff-necked' and 'uncircumcised in heart and mind' that they had failed to fully appreciate what the coming of Jesus highlighted and emphasised: namely, that 'the Most High does not dwell in houses made with human hands' (Acts 7:48).[5] William Barclay nicely sums up what Stephen was saying in this part of his speech by noting that he '. . . insists that they [the Jews] have wrongly limited God. The Temple, which should have become their greatest blessing, was in fact their greatest curse; they had come to worship it instead of worshipping God. They had ended up with a Jewish God who lived in Jerusalem rather than a God of all people whose dwelling was the whole universe.'[6]

Thought questions:

1. The Jews offer us a striking and sobering example of how people can prioritise buildings over God. In what way do you think that you or your church might do the same?
2. In what ways do we try to put God in a box?
3. Paraphrasing the quote from Barclay that came at the end of this section, how might we be in danger of producing an Adventist God who lives in Adventist accommodation, rather than a God of all people whose dwelling is the whole universe?

4. Often texts are quoted to support the concept that God remains the same: for example, Malachi 3:6, where He says, 'For I the LORD do not change. . . .' While God evidently does not change in the way He shows love, mercy and grace, He clearly changes His methods; this is seen especially in what He has accomplished through Jesus. How might this in turn be reflected in our ability to change and adapt to different circumstances?

Being God's Dwelling Place: Part II

So what of the way of thinking that Jesus initiated? The apostle Paul writes about God dwelling in us in three ways, each of which will be explored in turn. Firstly, he tells us about how God dwells in Christians on the global level. In his letter to the Ephesians, Paul is generally understood to be writing about this Church, which is purposely identified with a capital 'C'. This is the Church to which Christians everywhere belong. It is not any particular denomination or organisation, but God's Church, as established by Him on earth. Ellen White, while writing about the concept of Church as found in Ephesians, describes it like this: 'The children of God constitute one united whole in Christ, who presents His cross as the centre of attraction. All who believe are one in Him.'[7]

In Ephesians 2:19-22, Paul graphically draws a picture of this Church for us. It is almost as if he is mentally building the Church in his mind's eye as he writes: 'So then you are no longer strangers and aliens, but you are citizens with the saints and also members of the household of God, built upon the foundation of the apostles and prophets, with Christ Jesus himself as the cornerstone. In him the whole structure is joined together and grows into a holy temple in the Lord;

in whom you also are built together spiritually into a dwelling place for God.'

Starting with the foundations, Paul eventually arrives at a description of a spiritual building that is a spiritual dwelling place; for it is here that God lives. This is not a description of how an institution or organisation has come about, but of how people have been brought together. This can be seen in the way that it involves the gathering together of two distinct groups that are identified by Paul in the passage quoted above. One of the groups is described as 'strangers' and 'aliens'. These are the Gentile Christians: those people who were incorrectly and inappropriately kept at a distance by the Jews. Paul has expanded on this group in what has come previously, describing them as the 'uncircumcision' (Eph. 2:11); and explains that they were 'without Christ, being aliens from the commonwealth of Israel, and strangers to the covenants of promise' (Eph. 2:12). In other words, they were those people who were not privileged and destined to have had the Messiah come among them, and who were not aware of or benefiting from the promises made to Israel.

The second group are the Jews themselves, and they were definitely benefiting from the promises made to God's people. Paul describes them as those who have been chosen (Ephesians 1:4), adopted (Ephesians 1:5), and inheritors (Ephesians 1:11, 14). The reason that these are clearly understood to be the Jews is that any of Abraham's descendants reading or listening to Paul's letter would immediately have identified themselves as belonging to this group, because these were buzzwords embedded deep into their national consciousness and psyche. Just as the terms 'clan', 'glen' and 'loch' can make a Scot go misty-eyed, these words would be similarly emotive. For Paul's listeners would instantaneously be transported back to Haran, where God chose to give promises to their father Abraham. In choosing Abraham, God also adopts and chooses Abraham's offspring, offspring to whom He would give the land of Canaan (Gen. 12:7). The Jews' inheritance consisted not just of the promises themselves, as given by God, but also the land of milk and honey and their status as God's representative people on earth. As God Himself is reported as saying: 'For you are a people holy to the LORD your God; the LORD your God has chosen you out of all the peoples on earth to be his people, his treasured possession.' Deuteronomy 7:6.

Words of privilege indeed! Therefore, all Jews at the time Paul was writing to the Ephesians would know that he, Paul, was tugging at the heartstrings, zooming in on the core of their identity as God's people through the words he selected to describe them. And so, according to Paul, these two groups, the Gentiles, (the strangers and aliens) and the Jews (the chosen, adopted, inheritors) have been brought together by God through Christ in Ephesians.

These two groups are united because both have been brought into the household of God together. The building work commences by Paul noting that the foundations are based upon the work of the apostles and prophets: a group that includes the apostle Paul himself, of course, according to Ephesians 1:1. But, crucially, it is Christ as the cornerstone that ties the whole construction together and is the means by which a holy temple or dwelling place for God is established with no dividing walls.

The implications of what Paul is writing here are perhaps easy to miss or even to fully do justice to. It is astounding

that the Church – that is, Christians everywhere – is itself a spiritual entity, a united humanity where God can reside. Christians on a global level can be thought of as a spiritual building – a building where they, metaphorically speaking, form its very fabric. As the Phillips translation puts verse 22 of Ephesians 2, 'You are all part of this building in which God himself lives by his spirit.' The many are joined together by God's actions through Jesus and the Spirit, to be one dwelling place. It is therefore an amazing picture of spiritual unity that is being described for us here (see also Ephesians 4:3 to 6, 13, 15 and 16).

Our understanding of this spiritual unity is further enhanced by Paul, who lets us know that the spiritual building being described is actually unique. There is only one building of this kind, as there is just the one global Church. Paul does not go on to describe a global Church that is fragmented. Rather, the countless Jewish and Gentile believers are drawn together to collectively form a single place for God to dwell. We, who are Christians, are thus part of a spiritual community that encircles the entire planet.

Global Level	The Worldwide Christian Community	Ephesians 2:20-22 'a holy temple . . . a dwelling place for God'

On the next level, Paul writes about God dwelling in the

local church – that is, a church that is a specific Christian community in a particular location. To distinguish from the global Church that is written with a capital 'C', local churches are referred to hereafter as 'church' with a lowercase 'c'. In his first letter to the Corinthians, Paul is writing about just such a church. In 1 Corinthians 3:1-15 he describes the church planting of Apollos and Paul that led to the establishing of a Corinthian church, which is thought to have been composed of a number of house-group churches that occasionally met together.[8] In contrast to his letter to the Ephesians, here Paul uses the more earthy and organic metaphor of a growing plant to make his point about the local church's germination and maturation. Emphasising that it is God who is actually responsible for growing the churches in verse 6, Paul goes on to say in 1 Corinthians 3:16: 'Do you not know that you are God's temple and that God's Spirit dwells in you?'

Now, what is hidden from view in most translations is that when Paul refers to 'you' here, he is referring to all of the Christians at Corinth – it is therefore a collective 'you'. Furthermore, when he makes reference to a 'temple', he is writing about just the one temple. Hence, the verse can be read as saying: 'Do you [all the Christians at Corinth] not know that [all of] you [together] are God's temple and that God's Spirit dwells in [all of] you?'

Again, the same pattern is seen from when Paul wrote about the global Church in Ephesians. The local Christians, who are the local church, are joined together to comprise the one temple. It is again a spiritual unity that is being described – a unity that in turn becomes a dwelling place for God in the form of the Holy Spirit: but this time on a local level.

Local Level	Local Christian Communities	1 Corinthians 3:16 'God's temple' in which 'God's Spirit dwells'

So having established that God dwells in Christians globally and locally, the picture is completed by looking at how God also dwells in us individually. First Corinthians 3:16 and 1 Corinthians 6:19, 20 are very similar, but Paul is actually making two different points in these passages. Rather than talking about church planting, as he does in chapter 3, Paul in chapter 6 is writing about the much more personal subject of sexual ethics. It therefore makes sense that, here, he is referring to Christians as individuals, rather than as a group or collective. Paul suggests that the individual members that make up the global and local communities are themselves also temples, writing: '. . . do you not know that your body is a temple of the Holy Spirit within you, which you have from God, and that you are not your own?' 1 Corinthians 6:19.

So what Paul describes here is the culmination of an amazing and radical change: a change that has seen God move from dwelling in a building in the desert and then a building in Jerusalem, to dwelling in people spiritually on three levels.

| Global Level | The Worldwide Christian Community | Ephesians 2:20-22 'a holy temple . . . a dwelling place for God' |

| Local Level | Local Christian Communities | 1 Corinthians 3:16 'God's temple' in which 'God's Spirit dwells' |

| Individual Level | Christians | 1 Corinthians 6:19 'temple of the Holy Spirit' |

It is like the adoption of a new operating system that transforms the way things work. It helps us move from being focused on just one specific location to many, from four walls to countless people, from the tangible to the intangible. The manner in which God dwells among us may seem quite bewildering, its scope and breadth ranging from

everyone to one specific individual, from the Church to every church. It should be noted and emphasised that Paul does not suggest that God dwells in any sense in any particular building or buildings. Any need for solidity and a permanent address is not fulfilled here. In fact, nowhere in the New Testament are terms for church, such as *'ekklesia',*⁹ 'temple', 'house of God' and so on, used to refer to an actual building. There is not a breeze block, belfry or flying buttress in sight. It is people, people, people all the way.

But you might still have a niggling thought at the back of your mind that church, in the sense of attending a service in a church building, is somehow special. This may seem to be what is being hinted at when Jesus says in Matthew 18:20: 'For where two or three are gathered in my name, I am there among them.' There are, however, two crucial things to take away from this verse in the context of this discussion. Firstly, the physical aspect that results in Jesus being among people is because they have *gathered together*, wherever they are, be it to worship, to serve others, or to fellowship. It is the congregating of people, not bricks and mortar, that is important here. People can gather in a tenement building in Glasgow or a luxury dwelling in the millionaires' resort of Sandbanks near Bournemouth, and in both cases Jesus will be there among them as they worship Him and serve on His behalf.

Secondly, the spiritual aspect is seen as being the important motivational factor for gathering. Get together, but, for Christ to be present in a special way, get together in Jesus' name. That God is with His people in a special way when they come together should therefore be an encouragement to meet, not an encouragement to meet in a particular place or building. It is a call that should galvanise

us to meet together for the right reason . . . in the name of the One who died for us on Calvary and rose again so that we might have life, individually and collectively.

Thought questions:

1. How does the understanding that God dwells in people on three levels influence how you in turn understand what it is to be church?
2. If God's dwelling places are now all about people, not buildings, how does this influence our priorities from the perspective of people and church buildings?
3. People are often heard to say, 'I don't need to go to church to be a Christian.' In the light of the above discussion, how might you respond to that statement?

Being God's Dwelling Place: Part III

What does this all mean for the way that we think about and are church? In many a church building up and down the land, the words 'REVERENCE MY SANCTUARY' form the backdrop for the congregation. The capital letters, frequently used, almost demand compliance. This phrase is borrowed from either Leviticus 19:30 or Leviticus 26:2. 'Borrowed' is used purposefully, because at the time, of course, this referred to a literal sanctuary, and therefore a specific place or building. It is not possible for us to apply these verses to our present-day situation directly because God is not to be found in a tent in the desert or a temple at the centre of Jerusalem. For now it is all about God dwelling in people – right?

The trouble we have to mentally separate a church from the building it is associated with comes into play here. This is because the way we behave and think with regard to our churches often reflects the understanding that God dwells in buildings, not people. A not-so-infrequent sight is to see deacons move forward at the close of a service. Their job is to carefully and respectfully usher the congregation out so that the spiritual purity and integrity of the 'sanctuary' can be maintained. The irony is that, according to Paul, what they are really doing is directing the 'sanctuary', God's dwelling place at the local level, and the 'sanctuaries', God's dwelling place at the individual level, out through the door. For, if it is in the people that God dwells . . . what is left behind is an empty space.

The stern looks intended to police inappropriate behaviour, the shushes for quiet, the notions that this space is somehow a holy place, are not based merely on the congregation adhering to good manners or the need to be polite and maintain good order, but on a well-intentioned, but misconstrued, understanding that when we go to church we are entering an especially holy place, a sanctuary – a *building* in which God dwells.

Adventists are not alone in having adopted this thinking. Once the use of church buildings became established in early Christianity around the third century AD, 'sanctuary' was the name used to refer to the area around the high altar: the altar that was and is the most important among the many altars to be found in certain churches. This altar was and is referred to as being the 'high' altar because it is raised up and is therefore physically the highest altar. As with the sanctuary in Jerusalem, only the chosen few were and are historically allowed in this sanctified and holy area. This is where the priests perform their duties, especially the Eucharist or communion ceremonies. Anyone who has visited one of the cathedrals found in Great Britain, be it in Durham or Norwich, Wells or Lincoln, has seen the barriers stopping all and sundry from entering these areas. You and I are just not special enough for that, you see.

In religious circles the term 'sanctuary' is now commonly used to designate the place where people gather to worship God: even if there is no high altar, as is found in, among others, Catholic, Lutheran and some Anglican churches. The word 'sanctuary' sits comfortably with churchgoers because it is a biblical word that helps us to focus on the significance of worship and other church building-based activities. It can also sit comfortably with us when compared to other names for the places in which we worship. Especially so, as alternatives seem so jarring and congruent with secular activities: 'auditorium' is associated with the theatre and lectures; and 'worship space' can be thought to be too functional and nebulous. The 'church hall' is where we eat, have social activities and conduct Sabbath school classes. Frequently, it is called a sanctuary, because that is a way in which behaviour can be regulated. Call it something else, and the fear is that a free-for-all will occur; so 'sanctuary' it remains.

Yet, the issue at hand is not what we call a particular room, but the way that calling that room a 'sanctuary' in turn affects the behaviour and attitudes we display towards it. Through this we can lose sight of what is important and indeed biblical. Call it a 'sanctuary' and in practice it becomes a pseudo-sanctuary because of our perceptions and attitudes. Expectations are immediately put in place that elevate the place where worship occurs to a seemingly higher plane. The congregation is welcomed to the 'house of the Lord', forgetting that the congregation itself is that very house. The building and its spiritual and physical maintenance, rather than the people and their maintenance and upkeep, become our priority. The platform and pulpit can be given the same level of exclusivity and specialness as is seen with the furniture around high church altars: altars where special clothing and special attitudes are required of special people in order to maintain the appropriate level of 'holiness'. At times, in an Adventist setting and context, it is almost as if suits and ties are replacements for cassocks and robes – white shirts are as de rigueur as mitres.

Recalibrating one's mindset and language is not so easy, however. For Christians, some of the most evocative buildings to enter, from York Minster to Westminster Abbey, are those cathedrals mentioned earlier. Their beautifully stained glass windows, the lofty, soaring vaults, the amazingly decorative choir stalls, the music, the incense and the cool interior – even on the hottest of days – make them a sense-saturating experience. There is little doubt that architecture can contribute towards one's worship experience, which can easily lead us to think that as surely as the Queen is to Buckingham Palace, God is to such fitting and awe-inspiring settings. To drag one's attention away from carefully hewn marble and intricately carved wood to the people wandering in and out of the doors because these are the ones in whom God dwells – well, it just seems wrong.

The challenge here is to come up with a new vocabulary, a new way of talking about the Church and churches. To develop a way of thinking about church that is focused on the people, rather than the buildings in which they worship. To communicate to others and ourselves that people are our priority, because people are God's priority. How can we fully verbalise what it means for God to dwell in us globally, locally and individually? Contemplate what it might mean to reverence God through the way we treat the people in whom He dwells.

Thought questions

1. How can church be thought of more as a community of people as opposed to a building?
2. How might our language and the way we talk about church be changed to emphasise church as a community of people more than might currently be the case?
3. Given the discussion above about the changes Christ's coming made to the concept of God's people, what should reverence mean, and to whom is that reverence directed?

God and Being Church

Perhaps there is something surprising and liberating about

the way in which Paul discusses the Church in Ephesians. Until it was pointed out to me I had missed it. Paul is not writing about the Church as it should be, *but as it is*. Let that sink in for a moment. Paul is not explaining what needs to happen in order for the Church or churches to be: he is describing the Church and churches as God has already created them. It is therefore not something that we have to develop, manufacture or synthesise – God has already done what needs to be done.

The three texts quoted that refer to the three ways in which God dwells in His people do not say, 'God *will* dwell in us,' or that we will become part of the body of Christ, and so on, but rather that the Church *is* the body of Christ. Such is the situation now; it does not depend upon what we *will* do, but what God *has* done. This should come as such a relief. No longer is it necessary or even theologically appropriate for us to sit with furrowed brow and perplexed looks, trying to figure out how to get a church to be united. The God-created unity that is the Church is already in existence – we just need to partake in it. The unity that is found in a church is not something to be manufactured, but is something in which to join.

Now it should be noted here that there is a world of difference between joining in with something and just joining something . . . and this is not just playing with words. It is the difference between participation and mere enrolment. It is to do with the contrast between becoming a member of the RAC or the AA and working for the RAC or the AA. One is about being part of something, the other is about just benefiting from that same thing. It is the difference between sitting in a pew having fulfilled all the membership requirements, and, by contrast, living the reality of church – of growing to become a vital component of a Spirit-led community of believers. It is the contrast between understanding that church is something that spiritually feeds and nurtures us, and the notion that church is us.

With so many cultures, people groups and nationalities in our churches in Britain now, one of the common themes promoted is unity through diversity. This is often based on the idea that diversity can be maintained and indeed encouraged, but without fragmentation. This ideal already exists . . . because of what God has achieved and created through His Son and the Holy Spirit. It is a unity in which one can immerse oneself and engage with others. It is something that should fundamentally affect the way we relate to the Church and our churches. It is a unity that has already brought together such disparate, segregated and hostile groups as the Jews and Gentiles . . . you and I just need to get on board and enter into that unity that Christ has already created.

Thought questions

1. How might the concept that Church already exists, rather than being something that needs engineering, affect the way in which unity through diversity is addressed?
2. How would you describe someone who participates in the God-created unity that is Church and churches?
3. How much diversity can be tolerated without fragmentation occurring: or do God's unifying actions render this question redundant?

Jesus and Being Church

Going back to the drawing-a-picture-of-church exercise, a

legitimate way to respond to the question as to what one imagines when thinking of 'church' is simply to draw Jesus. It is telling that the letter to the Ephesians, which is so much about the Church, is saturated with references to Jesus Christ. There is no getting away from the concept that the Church and Christ are intimately linked. This is particularly seen in the way in which Paul uses the phrase, 'in Christ', and in the metaphors or word pictures describing the Church that he provides.

In terms of frequency, Paul uses the phrase 'in Christ' in Ephesians more than in any other of his works. This should immediately get our antennae quivering and brains buzzing when it comes to the task of considering just what the Church is about. These are not vain repetitions. The phrase 'in Christ' is important because it emphasises and shows that the way in which a number of things are accomplished can only be because of Jesus. The non-exhaustive list of these given below also demonstrates the scope of what Paul is suggesting is achieved in Christ.

- God has 'blessed us *in Christ* with every spiritual blessing in the heavenly places' (1:3).
- God has chosen 'us *in Christ*' (1:4).
- The Jews have '*in Christ* . . . also obtained an inheritance' (1:11).
- God, having made us, both Jew and Gentile, alive together with Christ (2:5), 'raised us up with him and seated us with him in the heavenly places *in Christ Jesus*, so that in the ages to come he might show the immeasurable riches of his grace in kindness toward us *in Christ Jesus*' (2:6, 7).
- God has 'created [us] *in Christ Jesus* for good works, which God prepared beforehand to be our way of life' (2:10).

- 'But now *in Christ Jesus* you who once were far off have been brought near by the blood of Christ' (2:13).

Very practically, it is in Christ, and therefore because and through Him, that God has sought to make the Church the way it is: a spiritual community composed of a diverse group whose lives have been transformed and, as we shall explore later, who are partaking in God's mission. Paul expands the concept for us further by describing the Church as the body of Christ in Ephesians 1:23. It is a familiar concept because Paul uses it in a number of ways in a number of places other than the one found in Ephesians.[10] It is this metaphor that Paul uses to portray the spiritual unity that is the Church, a unity in diversity. As Reinder Bruinsma suggests when referring to the metaphor of the body as found in Ephesians 4:5, 6: 'The body is unified because it is united in the Spirit and in the fundamental truths of the Christian Faith: "One Lord, one faith, one baptism: one God and Father of all, who is over all and through all and in all." '

The images that show how intimately Christ should be associated with the Church keep on coming. To ensure that Jesus' role is further understood, Paul describes Jesus as the Head of the body (Eph. 4:15). This image helped describe to Paul's first-century readers two things. Firstly, it emphasised how Jesus as the Head of the Church (see Eph. 1:22) provides leadership. Secondly, because the head was believed to be responsible for nourishment, Christ is shown to be a source of spiritual sustenance and is therefore the means by which and through which the Church grows. Paul informs us that one of the ways that Christ sustains and nourishes the Church is through the gift of ministries in Ephesians 4:11-13: 'The gifts he gave were that some would be apostles, some prophets, some evangelists, some pastors and teachers, to equip the saints for the work of ministry, for building up the body of Christ, until all of us come to the unity of the faith and of the knowledge of the Son of God, to maturity, to the measure of the full stature of Christ.'

It is striking that the gifts are not for personal satisfaction or contentment, but for the benefit of others, thereby contributing towards their spiritual maturity. George R. Knight brings this all together nicely by suggesting that the New Testament conveys the idea 'that the entire church is a . . . charismatic community'.[11] It is charismatic in the sense that the church as a whole is gifted, which helpfully brings us to a collective and not just an individual perspective.[12]

The second metaphor for the Church has already been discussed, because it is the metaphor of the temple in which God dwells and is the one that is found in Ephesians 2:15-22. But even here, Christ is portrayed as having a pivotal role to play, as He is described as the Cornerstone or Keystone (see Eph. 2:20). There is some debate among the scholarly community as to which is the correct translation, but both options fundamentally suggest how important Christ is for the well-being of the Church. For if 'cornerstone' is the correct translation, this is not only the first stone to be laid, but also the squarest and the biggest and therefore the one that greatly and profoundly influences the whole structure. If this stone were 'off' – misaligned in some way – then the whole edifice would be out of kilter. Alternatively, if Paul's intention was that Christ is to be regarded as the 'keystone', then this is still telling us how crucial He is to the success of the building. The keystone is the one that is found in the centre of an arch, and it is this stone that binds the structure together and completes it.

Paul's description of the Church in Ephesians is therefore laden with imagery that is closely associated with Jesus: which challenges us, as members of the body of Christ, to let those to whom we reach out see us as a Christ-saturated Church. This is where it all becomes extremely challenging. We are very comfortable in arriving at such a deep understanding of what the Church is all about; it's familiar Sabbath school class territory after all. The test comes when trying to ensure that a Christ-saturated church is more than just a theological construct or academic concept. The bottom line is, if someone walks into our churches off the street, will they see Jesus?

Thought questions:

1. What should be the characteristics of a church that has fully embraced what it is to be grounded in, founded on and built by Christ?
2. How can a church that is all about Jesus be all about Jesus to those who are part of that church community?
3. When people come into contact with a Christ-saturated church, how does that church reveal Christ?

The Spirit and Being Church

The role of the Holy Spirit in the Church must not be forgotten and has already been mentioned in what has been discussed previously. Referring again to 1 Corinthians 3:16 and 1 Corinthians 6:19, 20 it can be seen that it is specifically the Spirit that dwells within us locally and individually. The famous passage on unity found in Ephesians 4 expands upon the Spirit's function in this regard, where Paul writes: 'There is one body and one Spirit, just as you were called to the one hope of your calling, one Lord, one faith, one baptism, one

God and Father of all, who is above all and through all and in all.' Eph. 4:4-6.

With the key contributions that God and Christ make to the church already clear, it is important to understand how the Spirit's role also emerges as we progress through the letter. This role includes the key task of revealing what has previously been a mystery to us (Eph. 3:5). Paul suggests that there are two dimensions to this mystery. Firstly, that of Christ and the mystery of the incarnation and how this supreme act of sacrifice fits into the second mystery, which is God's plan itself: a plan that, according to Ephesians 1:9 and 3:9, remained a mystery until the Spirit's act of revelation. In Ephesians 3:16, Paul reveals that the Spirit is also involved in strengthening 'your inner being with power'.

Hence, the Spirit can be seen to have a very active role in the Church – through being present, through enabling us to understand what God's will is, through the sustaining and empowering of individuals, and the continual joining of those individuals together in a spiritual community. Thus the Church can be seen to be something that actively involves the whole Trinity; with God, Christ and the Spirit implicated in its creation, development, growth and ongoing existence. Paul helps the reader understand that this is the case very early on in his letter to the Ephesians. In chapter 1, verses 3 to 14, Paul offers a prayer of blessing, and in the final two verses he draws all this together neatly by writing:

'In him [Christ] you also, when you had heard the word of truth, the gospel of your salvation, and had believed in him, were marked with the seal of the promised Holy Spirit; this is the pledge of our inheritance toward redemption as God's own people, to the praise of his glory.' (Ephesians 1:13, 14.)

Perhaps it is difficult to see on a day-to-day basis that the Church is so bound up with all three members of the Godhead – that it is a spiritual entity rooted in and powered from above. As you walk in through the front door of your local church building on a Sabbath morning, experiencing the Trinity in all its fullness can be problematic when you are 'merely' setting up chairs, giving out hymnbooks or even partaking in the service. This is, however, what is so radical and amazing about the picture of the Church at the global level and of a church at the local level that Paul paints in the New Testament: in particular, that God would choose such a seemingly flawed and, at times, broken people in which to dwell and through which to fulfil His mission in the world. It is this latter aspect of the Church and God's mission that we turn to next.

Thought questions:

1. How can we allow ourselves to be more and more led by the Spirit? How might we perceive that we have the Spirit's leading if we do?
2. Do you perceive that your spiritual gifts are being used to build up the church? If not, what steps could you take to address this situation? If they are, what could be done to further enhance your contribution?
3. How might the different members of the Trinity allow us to conceive of different aspects of the Church that in turn will help us reach out to different people?

[1] Frank Viola and George Barna, *Pagan Christianity? Exploring the Roots of Our Church Practices* (Carol Stream, IL: Tyndale House Publishers, Inc., 2010), p. 10.
[2] See also Deuteronomy 12:11; 14:23; Ezekiel 37:26-28.
[3] Karl Barth, *Church Dogmatics: Volume 2 - The Doctrine of God Part 1 - The Knowledge of God* (Edinburgh: T & T Clark Ltd, 2000), p. 480.
[4] Ellen G. White, *The Desire of Ages* (Nampa, ID: Pacific Press Publishing Association, 2006), p. 165.

[5]'In fact it has been further suggested that '[t]he idea that God could be confined to a temple was a heathen idea, fitting for those whose god was a mere idol of stone.' John Phillips, *Exploring Acts: An Expository Commentary* (Grand Rapids, MI: Kregel Academic, 2001), p. 140.

[6]William Barclay, *The Acts of the Apostles* (Louisville, KY: Westminster John Knox Press, 1976), p. 69.

[7]Ellen G. White, *Selected Messages*, vol. 3 (Hagerstown, MD: Review and Herald Publishing Association, 2006), p. 21.

[8]This is thought to be the case due to verses such as 1 Corinthians 14:23. For more information on the nature of the early Church, see: Valeriy A. Alikin, *The Earliest History of the Christian Gathering: Origin, Development and Content of the Christian Gathering in the First to Third Centuries* (Leiden, The Netherlands: BRILL, 2010), p. 50.

[9]This is the Greek word normally translated 'church' in our English-language Bibles.

[10]See also Romans 12:5; 1 Corinthians 12:12-27; Colossians 1:18, 24.

[11]George R. Knight, *Exploring Galatians and Ephesians* (Review and Herald Publishing Association, 2005), p. 242.

[12]*Charisma* is Greek for 'gift'.

SECTION 2

Being Missional

Perhaps the most notorious example of a company's mission statement is that of Fujifilm, whose employees were to do everything in their power to 'Kill Kodak'. Alternatively, more positive examples are Walt Disney's mission to 'Make people happy' and Virgin Atlantic Airways' aim to 'Embrace the human spirit and let it fly'. Such statements are simple, clear, and clearly understood. Anyone working for these companies is completely aware of what they are trying to achieve as they walk into the 'office' on a Monday morning. Those who climb inside their Mickey Mouse costumes at the beginning of their work-shift know, as they plod up and down Main Street in Disneyland, that their prime role is simply to ensure that happiness reigns. The next time you are standing in line waiting to be seen at the Virgin Atlantic check-in desk, you can temper your frustrations by remembering that the staff are not simply allocating seats on planes, but also attempting to set you and others free!

However, are things that clear as you step through the door of your church building on a Sabbath morning? If a poll were conducted to find out why attendees were present that day, what would be their answers: spiritual refreshment, religious obligation, a thirst for community? Is it clear how and why each activity is taking place? What is being achieved, or, more pertinently, what is meant to be achieved as services are being faithfully attended, people are greeted at the door with a bulletin and a 'Happy Sabbath', Sabbath School lessons are debated and discussed, sermons are listened to and fellowship is experienced? How should the concept of the Church's mission, and consequently the mission of the local church, be understood?

Being Church and God's Mission

The way that Paul describes the Church in Ephesians, as being founded on, formed by, and in existence because of what God has achieved through Jesus and the Spirit, means that any sense of what a church's mission is must take this into account. Failing to do so would be like trying to understand an orchestra without taking into consideration the composer's score and the conductor's directions.

Further, thinking locally, it is important to understand whether churches are intended to be a means to an end, or an end in themselves. In other words, is God's mission fulfilled when churches are established and running, or do those same churches have something else to do or be? As we read through Ephesians it is evident that Paul was very creative and loved a metaphor or three. He introduces another one towards the end of the letter by making reference to a spiritual battle, writing:

'Put on the whole armour of God, so that you may be able to stand against the wiles of the devil. For our struggle is not against enemies of blood and flesh, but against the rulers, against the authorities, against the cosmic powers of this present darkness, against the spiritual forces of evil in the heavenly places.' Eph. 6:11, 12.

It therefore seems appropriate to carry this metaphor a little further. The idea that any given war is made up of many individual battles has led to Donald Trump's version of the familiar Chinese war strategist Sun Tzu's saying where he suggests: '. . . sometimes by losing the battle you find a new way to win the war.'

In many ways the local church can be seen to be fighting a battle . . . but let's hope that Trump's assertion that defeat may sometimes be necessary is not an essential feature of church life!

The key thing about battles is that they are part of something that is much, much bigger. Theories of combat suggest that battles should be thought of as a necessary part of an overall strategy – a strategy where the objective is to win the war. To get a view of the whole picture there are therefore two angles to consider: that which is represented by all the battles individually, and that which is provided by a bird's-eye view that enables the whole war to be accounted for. A war and its battles are intimately linked and so both need to be considered. It is not enough to just look at individual battles – which is a small-picture view. One also needs to take into account the bigger picture – that is, the war. As Paul suggests, this war has cosmic dimensions.

In Ephesians, Paul provides just such a big and a small

picture of God's mission for us to consider. The big picture is in view in the first chapter, where Paul tells us that from the very beginning of time or the 'foundation of the world' (1:4), God had plans to renew His broken and fractured creation. This is the overall strategy, the objective of the war, if you will. Such plans mean that He has been working towards a universal reconciliation of all things on heaven and earth (1:9-10). In a nutshell, what sin has damaged and divided, God is working to bring back together, to bring about healing so that things can be the way that He intended they should be. To continue the theme developed earlier, God is seeking to unite what has been torn apart because of sin.

We have already referred to the way in which Paul writes about Jews and Gentiles in his letter to the Ephesians. In the worldview of both Paul and his contemporaries there were only two types of people in the world: Jew and non-Jew, or, in other words, Jews and Gentiles. If you were not a Jew, you were, and indeed are, unquestionably a Gentile by default.

Paul uses the relationship between these two groups as a way of describing what God's mission is all about. He does this by describing for us the fractured status of the two groups as it was prior to Christ's coming. As we've seen, the Jews were those who were chosen (1:4) and adopted (1:5), and inheritors (1:11, 14): whereas all the others were 'aliens from the commonwealth of Israel, and strangers to the covenants of promise, having no hope and without God in the world' (2:12).

The relationship between the two groups was poor to say the least. Paul describes them as being radically separated, to the extent that he writes about them being 'far off' and with a relationship characterised as hostile (Eph. 2:13, 16). Ellen White suggests that the divide that existed between the two groups was driven by the Jews' need to be special, and so leading on to 'pride and exclusiveness'.[1] Never mind their responsibilities; they thought that being God's special and chosen people made them 'oh so superior'.

But that was then, and this is now. Then, they understood from Scripture that God dwelt among His people in a temple in the nation's capital; now, God through Christ has provided a radical makeover: because, now, the two groups are reconciled 'to God in one body through the cross' (Eph. 2:16). Now, all are 'citizens' and 'members' of God's household: a household that grows, as we have discovered, into a dwelling place for God. In a sinful world where the cracks and divisions between various people groups seem insoluble, God has stepped in. For God, through Christ, has '. . . create[d] in himself one new humanity in place of the two, thus making peace' (Eph. 2:15).

Such a division was not meant to be part of the original plan. When God picked out Abraham and his descendants in Genesis 12:3, the intention was that '. . . all the families of the earth shall be blessed.' The blessings that God was giving to Abraham and his offspring were in turn to be of benefit to all. Israel was not to be an exclusive club, but God's agent for change, reconciliation and a channel through which God's blessings would flow.

Because this plan failed to come to fruition, this meant that things moved on. Through the sending of His Son to die on our behalf, God, through the creation of a 'new humanity' (Ephesians 2:15), has ensured that previous distinctions between Jew and non-Jew no longer remain. Where once the Jews only were the inheritors, now the Gentiles too are heirs bound up in the same body (3:6). So the Church, as described by Paul, is the living, spiritual embodiment of a

united humanity that includes and encompasses both Jew and Gentile . . . again, in other words – everyone who is in Christ.

Where once, the nation of Israel was God's agent on earth and may well still have a specific part to play,[2] now there is a Church that is made up of all people groups. It is this Church that takes part in God's plan by being a place where God's unity is experienced, and by contributing towards bringing back together what sin has broken apart. Hence it's all about being a community of people where a God-created unity has become a living reality.

Thus, the Church's mission is intimately, inextricably linked to God's mission, or what Paul refers to as 'the eternal purpose that he [God] has carried out in Christ Jesus our Lord' (3:11). Rather than the Church needing a mission, God's mission needs a Church. God conceived of a people (Church) and a community (church) where the problems and fragmentation brought about by sin could start to be overcome. Hence, Paul tells us that it is 'through the church [that] the wisdom of God in its rich variety might now be made known' (3:10).

Ellen White describes this further for us by writing: 'The church is God's appointed agency for the salvation of men. It was organised for service, and its mission is to carry the gospel to the world. From the beginning it has been God's plan that through His church shall be reflected to the world His fullness and His sufficiency. The members of the church, those whom He has called out of darkness into His marvellous light, are to show forth His glory. The church is the repository of the riches of the grace of Christ; and through the church will eventually be made manifest, even to "the principalities and powers in heavenly places," the final and full display of the love of God. Ephesians 3:10.¹³

The Church, then, can be seen to function in two ways: firstly, as the human space where the spiritual unity that God has brought about can be found; secondly, as an institution to make God and His purposes known to those who are living apart, those who have a fractured existence because they are living lives outside of the unity that God desires for them and that the Church and churches represent.

This has a couple of implications. Firstly, the 1,001 different mission statements that various churches produce mean nothing if they are not aligned with and informed by God's mission. Secondly, everything a local church does must therefore be in harmony with God's mission – because that is why it was created and exists.

Thought questions:
1. Can one be a Christian without being involved in God's mission to bring about the unity to be found in a church?
2. Is your church's mission statement aligned with God's mission for the Church and churches? If you don't have a mission statement, what might it say?
3. How might your understanding of God's mission affect the way you relate to your church?
4. Being part of God's mission means more than just going to church services or stepping through the doors to your church building, as we never stop being a church. How might this thinking impact your life?

Being Missional: Practical Matters

One summer as a teenage student I worked in a pizza factory mixing pizza dough. Humping bags of flour and dough

around was extremely hard work – especially as the unusually hot weather perfectly complemented the ovens that were constantly pouring out inordinate levels of heat. To say that the environment was unbearably oppressive and sub-tropical at times would be an understatement. It was a great way to lose weight, but was not particularly great in any other sense. The drops of perspiration that poured off my face surely added that 'something extra' as at times they unavoidably fell into the mixer with the flour and water.

Several days into what turned out to be a morale- and strength-sapping job, the team I was part of were on a break. Slumped on the floor in the changing rooms, I was reflecting on how lectures would never again be regarded as boring and the life of a student unappreciated, when I was thrown a hairnet. In all my short time working for this company, I had seen no evidence of such an accessory, but now the whole workforce seemed to be donning them with unalloyed urgency. Not only that, but there was a definite atmosphere of quiet panic about the place.

I eventually found out that the local environmental health officer was making an unannounced visit to check that things were in order. Now, floors were being cleared and cleaned, hands washed and machinery wiped down. Where previously, the focus had been on getting as many pizzas through the door as possible, now food safety and quality were of prime importance . . . hence the hairnets.

Such attitudes have thankfully become outmoded, and so the food manufacturers that are successful now constantly focus on the quality and safety of their food, and not just the amount of food they produce. So, where once, an emphasis on high quality and food safety standards used to be a selling point when trying to encourage others to buy your product, more recently, such an attitude is just expected – it is the norm.

This change in attitude came about partly because of more rigorous checks being put in place by accrediting bodies, but mostly because attempting to put on a face on special occasions and for important visits just did not work. It was clearly the case that you were in danger of eventually being caught out.

However, there is more than a matter of consistency and its link to success going on here. Being consistent about something shows that that something matters. One-off efforts, as in the example above, do not convey the impression that food safety is of importance. Similarly, if God has created the Church and churches for His mission, and that mission is important, then being missional cannot just be a part-time activity.

Bringing things closer to home, let's pick on the concept of the visitors' day run by many of our churches. On one hand they are well-intentioned and they encourage members and attendees to pass around invitations. A special service is put on, the red carpet is metaphorically rolled out, and as a result the numbers in the congregation are often temporarily increased. On the other hand, however, it conveys the impression that visitors are only the church's focus on the occasion of just such a visitors' day. On all the other Sabbaths of the year, of course visitors are very, very welcome . . . but they are not exactly a priority.

Does that matter? Well if a church was created by God to fulfil His mission to put right the disunity brought about by sin, when doesn't it matter? One of the ideas behind visitors' day is that it encourages those not already in the church to be drawn towards the church. Thereby they are invited to become part of the church community and the unity it represents. That unity is not just about those already in the church becoming more unified, but about those outside the church also partaking in the unity that God has created in the church.

There are a number of similar days that might appear in a church's calendar. To visitors' days, one can add evangelism days, outreach days and community-focus days. For all such days, extra effort is expended, best faces are put on and metaphorical 'hairnets' are donned. Such a lack of consistency can communicate that we care about such things occasionally . . . but not consistently. It's a part-time approach to doing what God wants us to do and be concerned about all of the time. It's thinking about church as a series of programmes rather than a process or a state of being.

Perhaps the biggest reason for embracing one-off occasions is that the effort expended on special days is unsustainable. However, a bit of self-reflection might also identify a tendency to aim for inner contentment rather than an external focus. For the majority of the time we are content to muddle through, content to just do church primarily or even exclusively for ourselves. Content to be content. The danger is that the mission of such churches, in reality, becomes all about conducting services that are run by Adventists for Adventists to keep Adventists happy; or at least, if we're honest, 'happyish'. If things need to be different to reach out to the local community, it is not uncommon to hear it suggested that Sabbath morning is ring-fenced for 'us', and so let's see about doing stuff for 'them' later. Attention to both groups becomes compartmentalised.

This same compartmentalisation can be seen in the way in which evangelism in general is approached. Evangelism is often managed by a personal ministries or church growth department. The very fact that it is called a 'department' means that it can be viewed by us as one activity among many. In the same way that the children's department runs things for the children and does not necessarily involve every attendee, the same is often the case when it comes to personal ministries. As one needs to have the spiritual gift of teaching children, so it is with evangelism, it is thought – it is not a task for all, just for those who have been trained, the gifted, the keen and the coerced.

Thus, you have a few hardy souls with the necessary talents, or at least an indispensable evangelistic fervour, turning out on a Sabbath afternoon to doggedly go door-to-door, hand out leaflets or push magazines into letter boxes. On a larger scale, it is a similar situation that we see on visitors' day. The whole church can cope with an annual evangelistic series, but again such evangelistic initiatives are things that happen alongside church and are not routinely found at the core of who and what a church is. Personal ministries departments and evangelism initiatives comfortably sit outside the normal running of church. That this is the case is seen in the way that, if they do not happen, the church is

Evangelism

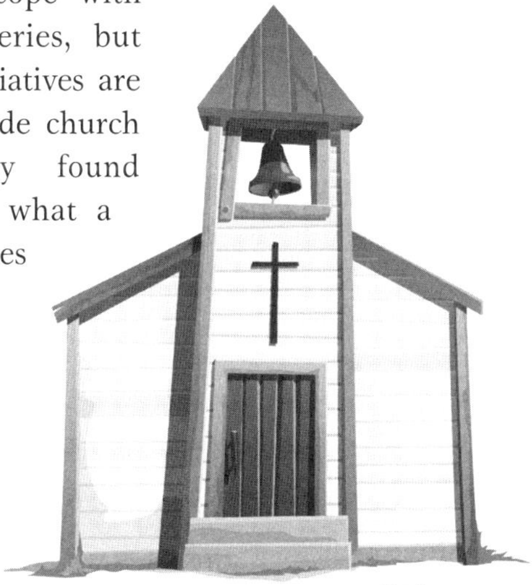

Fig. 1

Fig. 2

still seen to function: services are run, songs are sung, sermons are preached.

Such an attitude can be represented by figure 1. Evangelism in the form of the personal ministries department stands on the periphery of, or separate from, the day-to-day running of the church. However, given the understanding discussed above of what a church is about and for, it is inconceivable that any notion of trying to compartmentalise, in the way described, fits in with God's purposes for His churches. If it is acknowledged that a church is created by God, for God's purposes, and to aid in fulfilling God's mission, there is no aspect of church – of being church – that can fall outside that paradigm. Everything about a church must be about unity and therefore community, and its role in bringing Christ to those not yet in that community. Church growth needs to be something that is located at the core of the church, something that is central to a church's existence (see fig. 2).

Thought questions

1. Can a church function in a way that does not include God's mission?
2. If your answer is no, what about our churches where God's mission is at best a part-time activity?

3. As discussed above, this may be a language issue. As soon as you refer to something as a department then it just becomes one of many other departments. How might this problem be overcome?
4. How can church growth be a church's central concern?

Being Missional: Focus

Ever tried to speak to someone when they quite clearly would rather be watching the TV? Their attempts to keep their eyes trained on you as you talk to them are half-hearted, even though they may be well-meaning. You want to discuss what to have for dinner, but they seem to be more interested in what a complete unknown is cooking for a group of other unknowns on *Come Dine with Me.* You are desperate to sort out your holiday destination for the coming year, yet they are clearly judging the vocal talents of a contestant on the latest TV singing competition. Even though they have a vested interest in menu decisions and vacations, their focus simply lies elsewhere. Hence, actions in the form of contributions to the discussion are limited at best.

We, as members of a church community, can often be similarly distracted and well-meaning at the same time. An interesting exercise is to consider where your church's attention is. In what direction do the people who comprise your church primarily have their focus? What follows are three suggestions as to how a church's focus might in turn affect its behaviour. For, in the way that someone's focus affects their actions, the same can be seen to be true for a church. The first option to consider is a church that completely or mostly focuses on itself and its internal needs. This is represented by the diagram in figure 3.

Fig. 3: Navel-gazing orientation

Such a focus can potentially result in the following behaviour:

• The church is treated as something separate from the members – a third-party entity with a life of its own.
• The focus is inward, on maintaining the church (the entity) as it is.
• The majority of effort is put into keeping the existing membership happy.
• Little effort is directed outwards towards the local community or evangelistic activities.
• The primary mission objective is to evangelise the children of members.
• The primary aim is to keep everything as it has always been, and comfortable.

Another extreme is a church whose primary focus is outwards. This is represented as follows:

Fig. 4: Outward gazing

The characteristics of such a church are:

- The primary focus is on those who are not yet in the church.
- The tendency is to target numerical growth to the exclusion of organic growth.
- Little effort is directed at those in the church; they are merely resources with which to reach out.
- Change is governed by the needs of those outside, not inside the church.

A final concept is one that takes into account that the church is a God-created spiritual community brought about for the purpose of partaking in God's mission. This is represented in figure 5.

Fig. 5: Church in community

Such a church will:
- Seek to embody what it means to exist as a spiritual community.
- Focus holistically on both those inside the church and those who are yet to be in the church.
- Look out from within community.
- Talk to both those inside and outside the church to both find out what their specific needs are and respond accordingly.
- Allow God's mission to inform every aspect of the church.

A relatively recent term for describing this last category of church is 'missional'. It is important to understand that a missional church does not just do evangelism or conduct personal ministry activities, but is what it says on the tin . . .

missional. So, 'missional' is not just a label, brand or buzzword, but refers to something much, much deeper. It is like the familiar seaside confectionary, rock candy, that is not only perilous for the teeth but has 'Brighton' all the way through. No matter how many bites you take, or which aspect of it you look at, a missional church will always have its 'missionalness' on display.

It's like the difference between someone who just sings and someone who is a singer. Now I've sung in choirs and other musical ensembles, so would consider myself generally able to carry a tune. However, the full inadequacy of my singing voice hit home as I made use of the 'facilities' when attending a concert once. Apologies for the setting, but as my fellow restroomer and I washed and dried our hands, he was evidently warming up for the concert to come. A member of the world-famous St John's College Choir, Cambridge, his resonant and beautiful baritone voice filled the space in which we stood, and I confess to dawdling a bit so I could listen to him . . . despite the less-than-ideal surroundings. Since then, I have realised that I am someone who simply sings; there, in that not-so-salubrious environment, I had chanced upon someone who doesn't just sing, but is a singer.

This brings us back full circle to exploring the church in terms of what it is, rather than what it does. For such churches are defined by being missional, not by being churches that do mission. You cannot separate out God's mission from such a church's existence. A church that *does* mission is a church that can take or leave mission. A church that *is* missional has no choice but to be missional because that is the way that God has conceived it. Such a church has in every aspect of its existence and being taken into account the reason for which God created it in the first place.

Having a functioning personal ministry department or conducting some evangelistic initiatives such as 'campaigns', messy church, health expos or visitors' days does not mean that a church can claim to be missional. This is because it is a state of being, and so every aspect of a missional church is influenced by the part it plays in God's mission. A missional church is compelled by its very God-created nature to impact the lives of the communities it comes into contact with and the spiritual well-being of those who are already a part of the body of Christ. If this means adapting services, making the life of the church as accessible as possible by modifying language or even having comfortable chairs – then a missional church will do what needs to be done and be what it needs to be. If a missional church has bulletins, they will be missional bulletins; if it embraces small groups, they will be missional small groups.

This way of understanding what the Church should be came about because of the need to fully understand that the Church has been created by God and then sent by God 'to participate in the movement of God's love towards people'.[4] It recognises that not only are the God-created communities that are the Church and churches His initiative, but also that their reason for being is defined by God and Him alone. It puts to bed any idea that mission is what is done overseas, or involves simply saving individuals from eternal non-existence. It embraces what it is to be a church that participates in God's mission to seek reconciliation of all things on heaven and earth (Ephesians 1:21, 22). The logical conclusion to draw, and it's a disquieting one in many ways, is that if a church is not missional, it is not a church . . . it is at best dysfunctional or at worst a pastiche.

Thought questions

1. No church will be adequately described by any of the above models; however, which model does your church most closely resemble?
2. How might a church's point of view be changed?
3. Might it be better for a church to have many focuses or one – how might you favour one over the other?
4. How can being aware of what God's mission is all about help bring a more biblical focus to the way your church conducts itself?

Being a Missional Church

So what are the practical differences between a church that is missional, and a church that does mission or merely has some evangelistic activities as part of its programme? What might a church that attempts to see its role as a community partaking in God's mission look like? There are a number of characteristics that can be identified in answering these questions, and these are discussed in turn below.

Intentionality

It might seem obvious, but one of the characteristics of a missionally oriented church is that it has a missional mindset and thinks intentionally about mission. In many ways this is simply a case of a church community asking itself *how* it can fulfil its role as a spiritual community involved in God's mission. An example of this is where Christchurch (our second case study), in thinking about this aspect of who they are, said that their intention is:

'. . . to really connect people in that way of wanting to really help people become better disciples of Jesus. So being disciples of Jesus is not just about increasing our knowledge about God, but actually in some ways we know through doing as well. And so we would want to encourage people into that activism of their faith as well.'

Similarly, the Kingsgate members (as seen in our first study) want intentionality and:

'. . . want people to connect', 'to belong', 'to feel that the church is theirs', 'to be welcomed', 'to help people find their place'.

If you as a church are failing to achieve what God intends then things might need changing through critically assessing what you are currently doing. For Christchurch, this meant changing the way their small groups worked in a fundamental way. It is recognised that one of the weaknesses of small groups is that they can turn into 'holy huddles'. Such groups are prone to become very inward looking and one-dimensional. As David Cox puts it, 'They can create an atmosphere of exclusiveness, not inclusiveness, for those who do not belong to such a circle.'[5]

Christchurch responded to this potential pitfall by changing the structure of their groups. First of all they increased the size of the groups from the traditional 6 or so people to groups of 20 to 30. Secondly, they purposefully built into the way the groups were run the concept that they were to reach in, out and up. This is where 'reaching in' involves activities designed to develop the unity and fellowship seen among those who were already members of the groups. 'Reaching up' is the spiritual element that is aimed at encouraging group members to deepen their relationship with God; and would therefore include times of Bible study and prayer, for example. 'Reaching out' is what might be called evangelistic activity, but is more than that, and so involves seeking to take the Gospel in some form to those not yet part of the group. An advantage of having so many people in their not-so-small groups was that they were able to achieve much more than would normally be the case for the more traditional small group of 10 people or fewer.

This emphasis on a balanced approach both challenged and changed the existing culture by embracing a revitalised understanding of what it is to be church. In essence, what they are intentionally trying to do is create not just small groups, but missional small groups, or, as they term them, 'Connect Groups'. The thinking behind this was a shift in thinking where:

'The difference between a life group and a Connect Group is that Connect Groups have more of an outward focus.'

It is interesting how the label we put on things betrays our focus, in turn affecting their function and how they are perceived. 'Life group' is a common term that churches use to refer to their small groups and can have lots of positive connotations. However, Christchurch wanted a name for their new gatherings that reflected the balanced approach outlined above. 'Missional communities' was their aim, and also a name they flirted with. However, they decided that the term 'Connect Group' was user-friendly and described in much more familiar language what the groups were intended to be all about: namely, connecting to God, connecting to each other and connecting to those yet to be part of the group.

Kingsgate have a similar approach to that of Christchurch. They too are looking to encourage their small groups to reach in, out and up. Their structure is slightly different as they still have the more traditional small group or life group consisting of a handful of people. But these then gather together in clusters of five or so small groups, which enables them again to have enough resources to do more than just huddle together.

Sometimes it is just a case of asking yourselves the right question that encourages a missional outlook. For example, Christchurch are continually asking themselves:

'So actually how can we engage our friends with the Gospel? How can we engage them with what we're doing? How can we engage them with drawing them closer to Jesus?'

Similarly, every Monday, after the weekend activities, the Kingsgate leadership team meet to discuss how things went during that week's services. They ask themselves, what could we have done better and what might we need to change? Or, as they put it:

'So we're constantly . . . reviewing and analysing . . . "What did we do yesterday that might not have helped?" '

The key element to consider here is that they are doing it all the time. This is not just something such churches do for the odd occasional visitors' day, or visioning meeting, but regularly. This leads on to another characteristic to consider – consistency.

Consistency

As discussed above, being consistent about something shows that it is important to you. This aspect of being missional comes across very strongly in the way in which Kingsgate think. So, rather than having one-off visitors' days, Kingsgate are determined that: 'Every service that we do, every time, is geared towards welcoming and helping connect the people who are here for the very first time.'

And again: 'From the word go . . . every single Sunday,

every single service we run, we'll lead up front with [saying] we want to welcome new people and help people get connected.'

So there is a focus on constantly and consistently trying to allow those who come into their sphere of influence to connect to the church. In fact Kingsgate are so focused on visitors that they have developed what they term an 'invitational culture'. This is not just encouraging their church to invite their friends, family and colleagues on the occasional special visitors' day – which they still have, incidentally – but encouraging the congregation to always be thinking about whom they can invite to church events.

Perhaps the most notable example of how their invitational culture plays out in the life of the church was on the occasion of one of Kingsgate's Christmas services where they achieved a 100% uplift in attendance, seeing 4,000 people attend over the two services. However, this would not have happened if inviting people were an occasional effort. As Kingsgate themselves put it: '. . . if you haven't got an invitational culture, the whole of the year, for the whole of the church, . . . in the whole of the community, there is nobody to invite.'

That's a clear indication that reaching out through invitation is something that lies constantly and consistently in the heart of who Kingsgate are. But it is not just about being consistent in terms of inviting people; there is also a need to be consistent in what is on offer once those invitees step through the door. Therefore, everything is 'geared towards welcoming and helping connect the people who are here for the very first time'.

DNA

Another way of understanding the characteristics of a missional church is to consider its 'DNA'. In many ways this is a values-based approach where organisational values, according to Aubrey Malphurs, are 'the constant, passionate, sacred core beliefs that drive the ministry' of a church.[6]

A missional church will therefore have missional values – or, to put it another way, missional DNA. An example of this approach can again be drawn from the case-study churches: Kingsgate members purposefully seek to ingrain shared mission, vision and values. This is done by intentionally seeking to encourage: '. . . a culture and a place where people can get connected and helped and supported and encouraged wherever they are'.

It is informative that mention is made here of culture. Churches frequently go through a process of identifying their values, and these can often turn out to be a wish list. In other words they are the values a church would like to have, rather than the values that a church has in practice. The difference comes down to a church's DNA, or culture. The actual values that a church has are linked to its culture, the way it behaves and the way in which it finds meaning. A church, being a God-created spiritual community partaking in His mission, will inevitably find purpose and meaning in His plans. In other words, it is not any particular group's understanding of what their values are, but it is the adoption of values that are God-ordained, God-inspired, and God-designed, which were embodied and modelled for us in the person of Jesus Christ.

Thought questions:

1. In what way is your church similar or dissimilar to the

examples given above?

2. What other characteristics might a missional church exhibit?

3. Perhaps one of the hardest characteristics to display is consistency. What measures could be put in place, or attitudes encouraged, that might remedy inconsistency?

4. What steps might be taken to adopt and embrace values that are missing? How do communities guard against valuing traditions and systems above people?

[1] Ellen G. White, *Thoughts from the Mount of Blessing* (Hagerstown, MD: Review and Herald Publishing Association, 2000), p. 47.

[2] Referring again to Reinder Bruinsma's book about the Church, there are a number of Adventist scholars who believe there is an ongoing role for the Jews in God's purposes. For a discussion on this see: Reinder Bruinsma, *The Body of Christ: A Biblical Understanding of the Church* (Hagerstown, Maryland: Review and Herald Publishing Association, 2009), pp. 39–40.

[3] Ellen G. White, *Acts of the Apostles* (Nampa, ID: Pacific Press Publishing Association, 2006), p. 9.

[4] David Jacobus Bosch, *Transforming Mission: Paradigm Shifts in Theology of Mission* (Orbis Books, 1991), p. 390.

[5] David Cox, *Think Big, Think Small Groups: A Guide to Understanding and Developing Small Group Ministry in Adventist Churches* (Watford, Hertfordshire: South England Conference of Seventh-day Adventists, Department of Personal Ministries, 1998).

[6] Aubrey Malphurs, *Values-Driven Leadership: Discovering and Developing Your Core Values for Ministry* (Grand Rapids, MI: Baker Books, 2004), p. 10.

Being Accessible

Christ and Being Accessible

The temple at Jerusalem during Christ's day was said to be one of the wonders of the world at the time. While there were many features, such as doors covered in gold, the temple was predominantly made out of a white stone that was further bleached by the sun. On certain days, according to Jewish historian Josephus, the effect of the whiter-than-white stone was to make it look like the hill on which the temple was built was covered in snow. Walking up Temple Hill, rising above the streets of Jerusalem with the walls of the temple towering above you, must have been an awe-inspiring experience for first-time and regular visitors alike. Wandering through Solomon's Portico, with its multiple columns that offered welcome relief from the heat in the summer and shelter from the cold in the winter, you would eventually emerge blinking into the bright sunshine of the Court of the Gentiles. This court was purposefully designed to be big enough to accommodate vast swathes of worshippers and visitors.

It would have been fascinating to hang around and watch all of the comings and goings in this area. There would be those who were completing their cleansing rituals, others involved in selling and buying animals for sacrifice, the notorious moneychangers, curious foreigners, officious and overbearing Romans. The sights, sounds and smells would have made this a multi-sensory experience.

However, unless you were a Jew, this experience would be cut short. The journey towards the centre of the temple complex was a journey towards ever more sanctified areas. But located at a discreet distance from the area that contained the most important and sacred parts of the temple was a low wall or balustrade. Interestingly, there were no guards: just an ominous warning aimed at those who would dare to step through one of the many gaps in the wall. A copy of the warning statement was found in 1871 on a stone understood to have come from just that wall. The inscription, originally in Latin and Greek, reads:

> 'No man of another race is to enter within the fence and enclosure around the Temple. Whoever is caught will only have himself to thank for the death that follows.'[1]

For all non-Jews this would certainly have given them cause to stop and ponder! No pandering nanny state in evidence here; this was not a health and safety notice . . . but a clear threat. The most significant and sacred parts of the temple were off limits, literally out of bounds to anyone but the Jews. Paul, himself, experienced the gravity with which the Jews held and maintained the sacredness of the inner courts of the temple when, in the story found in Acts 21:27-36, he is accused by the Jews of taking the Gentile Trophimus beyond the barrier and 'into the temple' and so charged with having 'defiled this holy place'.[2]

Now, although these were trumped-up charges, Paul's life was in very real danger as he was dragged out of the temple and through that balustrade back into the Court of the Gentiles. It wasn't that the Jews were just considering killing him, but according to Acts 21:31 they were actually 'trying to kill him'. It is highly conceivable that Paul has this traumatic event in mind when writing the letter to the Ephesians. This is suggested for two reasons. Firstly, because this is where Trophimus was from.[3] Secondly, because most commentators understand that the 'dividing wall' that is mentioned in Ephesians 2:14 is the very wall that Paul was accused of breaching. Hence, Paul had first-hand experience of the hostility, exclusiveness and separation that the wall had grown to represent . . . even though he was a Jew.

Paul tells us in Ephesians that Christ has symbolically broken down this wall, and removed the barriers, real or otherwise, that symbolised and emphasised the distinctiveness that was thought to exist between Jew and Gentile. Now, because of Christ, both groups were free to be 'one new humanity in place of the two, thus making peace'.[4] Bringing Jew and Gentile together was an all-encompassing act – there was and is no one else living on earth – we are all either a Jew or a Gentile, remember.

Paul goes on to describe how both of these groups, in other words everyone, are now reconciled 'to God in one body through the cross, thus putting to death that hostility through it'.[5] This was a dramatic and powerful statement for

Paul to make at the time. It was the spiritual equivalent of bringing down the walls that split Belfast, Berlin and Nicosia all at once. For, as the inscription on that temple wall suggests, it was not just about segregation and distinctiveness, but would impact lives.

Thus, the brilliant picture that Paul paints for how Christ has opened things up and provided access to God for everyone is inspiring and heartening. The Church that Paul is thus describing is an open-access church: there are no locked doors, no barriers, and entry is open to all through Christ. As Ellen White suggests, 'Christ came to demolish every wall of partition, to throw open every compartment of the temple, that every soul may have free access to God.'[6]

Perhaps one of the most exclusive groups in the world, or so the American Express Corporation would have us believe, is made up of those of its customers who have an American Express black credit card.[7] To get your hands on one of these almost mythical slices of plastic, one needs to meet a number of strict criteria. Of course the biggest hurdle to overcome is getting an invitation to even apply in the first place, but other requirements mean that you need to have spent over £200,000 (250,000 US dollars) on other American Express cards, and paid a one-off joining fee of £2,500 (roughly 3,100 US dollars) and an annual fee of £2,200 (roughly 2,700 US dollars).[8] It is not surprising, then, that this card is for those who, broadly speaking, are known as being decidedly well off. You might consider the benefits worth it, and though they are never openly published they are thought to include automatic upgrades when flying, the use of a 24-hour concierge, the service of a personal shopper and access to tickets for sold-out events.

Such a world is utterly alien to that of the average, or even not-so-average, church-goer. It is purposely difficult to get the black credit card as the intention is to make it appealingly exclusive. You see, flashing this bit of plastic is a way of advertising that, in monetary terms at least, you are special.

Jesus breaking down the wall of hostility and allowing God and the Church to be accessible to all is like saying that the American Express black card is now available to all: even if you have not paid the joining fee. Imagine the chaos this would cause. Suddenly the VIP lounges at airports would be overflowing, the economy-class seats would be empty as everyone would be benefiting from the extra leg room in first class, and those personal shoppers would be overworked. Appropriately, Ellen White describes this opening up of the benefits of the Church and Christianity to all by suggesting that the breaking down of the wall of hostility let Jew and Gentile alike 'into the full privileges of the gospel'.[9]

Thought questions:

1. How does it make you feel and respond when you see the way in which God, through Jesus, has opened up the Church to all people?
2. What does an accessible local church community look like and how does it act?
3. In what ways might a church community, rather than having a positive influence, be a hindrance or even a barrier to those trying to connect to Jesus?

Being an Accessible Church

No local church is going to be 100% accessible. To be accessible to everyone all of the time in every place is obviously not only unworkable, but impossible. There are steps, however, that might be considered when thinking about how to ensure that the way that your local church runs and happens minimises the barriers it puts up between itself and others.

Communication Barriers

The clichéd idea that medical practitioners have terrible handwriting has been somewhat negated by modern technology. Instead of scribbling incomprehensible notes you'll never see, now they are typed as the consultation is in progress. Hence, it is part of the fun to try and get a glimpse of what is being recorded by peering nonchalantly at the computer screen. It is also fascinating to compare the language used in the notes to that used by the doctor when speaking to you, the patient. What might be recorded as the rather ominous-sounding 'peripheral oedema' would be swollen ankles to you and me. Similarly, DOE or dyspnoea is shortness of breath, and you should be very happy to see VSS on your notes as this means that your vital signs are stable. Even though doctors have a whole other vocabulary and shorthand they use on a professional level, when they speak to patients they employ everyday language to ensure that they are communicating clearly . . . because that is important to them and us.

There is general acknowledgement that churches have lots of in-house language, and so church-speak can seem just

as incomprehensible to 'outsiders' as do esoteric medical terms. In many ways this is a communication barrier that is so easy to fix and is so often identified as a problem; and yet it is hardly ever addressed. Just look at the customary order of service that has wording and phrases, often from Latin, that are essentially meaningless outside of that setting: 'doxology', 'benediction', 'invocation', 'recessional' and so on. The list of esoteric terms further encompasses everything from 'Sabbath School', via 'potluck', 'ingathering' and 'ordinances' through to 'divine service'.

You could suggest that it is just part and parcel of being involved in a new organisation. Every group has its own language and terms, and a church is just the same, surely. One of my previous jobs involved selling food to supermarket chains, and this, similarly, had its own lingo. It was imperative to quickly come up to speed on knowing and understanding about BOGOF (buy-one-get-one-free) and WIGIG (when-it's-gone-it's-gone) promotions; and of course GEs (gondola ends), POS (point of sale) and EDLP (every-day-low-pricing). It was a testing moment when a new TLA (that's a three-letter acronym, of course!) was thrown out and it was assumed that you, a professional in your field, should know immediately what it meant.

That is just the problem. The onus is on you, the new recruit or the outsider, to understand what they are talking about. In order to be included, you need to bring yourself up to speed, or sit there floundering as others talk above and around your head. Does a church need to be like that? Are we really prepared to say that those not yet in the church need to be prepared to understand us before they can start to be part of us? Is it necessary to hand out a glossary sheet explaining in-house terminology to visitors? Is it really a problem to change from announcing the 'benediction' to announcing a 'closing prayer'?

But even if you have eliminated such terms, only the surface has been scratched. What is missed by most of the attendees at a service at Kingsgate Community Church in Peterborough is the care and consideration that is put into their sermon preparation. Sermon scripts are run past a group of people who check the language and the way ideas are communicated. This includes both young and old 'evaluators' who point out obscure references to 1970s sitcoms or impenetrable theological words. Having received this feedback, the sermon is adjusted before being practice-preached before a panel of four of the church's staff on the Thursday. Even then, it might be changed, and only once this process has been gone through will the sermon be delivered on a Sunday.

One of the reasons for doing this is that Kingsgate strive to take great care with how they communicate biblical messages. Kingsgate want to ensure that the manner in which their sermons are put across is such that both the person who is present for the first time and the regular attendee are able to understand and be impacted. When the leaders of Kingsgate were interviewed, they emphasised that this does not entail 'watering down' the message. It is not about cutting and pasting and editing the sermon to the extent that it lacks substance and fails to do justice to what the Bible is trying to tell us. It is about ensuring that the language being employed does not act as a barrier to the message being conveyed.

Hence, attention is given to whether mention is being made of obscure or old cultural references such as *Dad's Army*, to which only people of a certain age can relate.

Although dense theological notions such as sin and the atonement might be meat and drink to some, these might also need explaining clearly and simply enough for visitors to grasp what is being said.

Christchurch London have a similar value. They talk about 'using good language', cutting down on 'Christianese'. Hence, instead of calling their small groups 'missional communities', they employ the term 'Connect Groups', because this is less threatening, uses more understandable in-house terminology and starts to explain in familiar language what the groups are all about.

Of course every group will unconsciously eventually develop its own in-house language, so there is the need to constantly review this aspect of church. However, being a church that makes its messages accessible will involve being aware of all language being employed: be it on websites and in blogs, or in bulletins, promotional literature, Facebook pages and Twitter feeds. Processes should be in place to ensure that the very language that is being used does not itself act as a barrier. Thus, being an accessible church means having accessible messages.

Ellen White also encourages us to put a great deal of care into the way in which we communicate to others. She notes that Paul was 'always shaping his message to the circumstances under which he was placed' and that we should 'study carefully the best method' to communicate to others in a winsome manner.[10]

Thought questions:

1. What are other examples of language that we might use in a church setting that can be difficult for visitors to comprehend?

2. According to research only 7% of the way in which we communicate is verbal, with the remainder being the tone of voice at 38%, and body language at 55%. In what way might these other forms of communication either be barrier-forming or allow others to access church?

Language Barriers – An Adventist Perspective

A final aspect of communication and language to consider is the issue that arises through the use of 'them' and 'us' language. As Adventists, we have our own language and culture and can seemingly readily identify those who are part of that culture. It is therefore very easy to slip into a 'them' and 'us' mindset. A big issue to take into consideration here is that this immediately sets up a barrier that is unconsciously or even consciously erected by 'us', and one that can be very much perceived by 'them'.

This has shown itself traditionally in the way in which we

refer to those 'outside' of Adventism as the 'world'. Additionally, this type of vocabulary can be used to distinguish between 'Christian' and 'non-Christian', 'Adventist' or 'non-Adventist'; and it is not that uncommon to hear the two groups described as 'sinners' and 'saints'. Recent attempts to develop a more acceptable language of difference have still resulted in distancing 'us' from 'them' by referring to 'them' as the 'community' or as 'the community people'.

Of course, there is a difference between someone who is and someone who is not an Adventist. However, this language of difference drives the assumption that Adventists are in some sense separate from the communities in which they live and worship. Adventists merely partake in the various aspects of the local community – shops, dentists, sports centres, parks and so on – as some sort of visitor. It is almost as if Adventists are walking around in a bubble until we meet fellow believers on Sabbath to unite in one big Adventist bubble. This is partly encouraged by familiar lines in songs such as 'This World Is Not My Home', which suggest that the planet we currently inhabit is but a temporary abode and that an eternal residency awaits for the chosen few in heaven, when in fact it is our home, though it will be made new according to Revelation 21.

Hence, the language of difference has implications for patterns of behaviour and thinking. Some might suggest that such a distinct separation is biblical. Recalling the familiar Christian slogan, 'Be in the world, not of the world', Romans 12:2 is cited in support, where it says: 'Do not be conformed to this world, but be transformed by the renewing of your minds, so that you may discern what is the will of God – what is good and acceptable and perfect.'

The Greek word, *aion*, rendered 'world' in the vast majority of translations, is a term from which the English word 'aeon' is derived. Here, Paul is telling his readers not to be conformed to the world by not giving in to the spirit of the aeon, or age. By the spirit of the age he is referring to its mores, values and standards. How this is to be accomplished is covered just a bit later in Romans 12:9-21. Paul suggests that this is not achieved by retreating from the firing line into a castle or fortress. Rather, Paul writes of the need to have genuine love, and hate what is evil (vs. 9); he encourages the Romans to love one another (vs. 10), and to 'extend hospitality to strangers' (vs. 13) and 'weep with those who weep' (vs. 15), and effectively summarises how to combat the spirit of the age by finally encouraging his readers to 'overcome evil with good' (vs. 21).

Paul is not suggesting that we wrap ourselves in bubble wrap so as to achieve splendid isolation. He is not encouraging the distancing of ourselves from those who are not like us. Rather, he encourages Christians to allow themselves to be renewed so as to combat the spirit of the age with good; to battle the trend for broken human relations through neighbourly love. Interestingly, this is a passage that also talks about the church as a body (see verses 4 and 5), and so reminds us that this is not just about individual effort, but that the church as a community is to battle the destructive spirit of the age.

Further insight can be found in Jesus' farewell speech to His disciples, found in the Gospel of John. This, again, is often quoted to support the idea that we are to be separate from our communities or the world. In John 17:14-18 Jesus is praying for His disciples and says: 'I have given them your word, and the world has hated them because they do not belong to the world, just as I do not belong to the world. *I am not asking you to take them out of the world*, but I ask you to protect them from the evil one. They do not belong to the world, just as I do not belong to the world. Sanctify them in the truth; your word is truth. *As you have sent me into the world, so I have sent them into the world.*'

There are a couple of things to take note of in this passage. In his Gospel, John writes about the 'world' with two major meanings in mind. As with Paul, here, for John, the 'world' in one sense does not represent the communities or the people among whom we live. Rather, the world here denotes the evil spirit of the age and the prevailing flawed and sin-affected system. It is a 'world' that is oriented towards and dominated by evil – a world that people need rescuing from, which is being ruled by Satan (John 12:31).

In other contexts in John's Gospel, however, the world is not something to be avoided or from which to escape, but is something to be loved as God loves it – most famously, of course, in John 3:16. The world is to be renewed, not destroyed, as we know from the picture John paints in Revelation 22. The 'world' in its other meaning in John is not the worldly system, but a vast community made up of human beings who desperately need to be reacquainted with divine grace and love. Here, again, Jesus is not making use of the language of isolation, but of sending; and we know from John 20:21 that God first sent Jesus, and He in turn has sent us.

There is therefore a distinction that emerges between those who have been sent and the target(s) of this sending. And so it is natural and inevitable to differentiate between those inside and those outside a church (yet another oft-used distinction). However, being aware of the barrier this sets up between 'us' and 'them' is crucial. For if we, the people, are the body of Christ, then what we can be doing in reality is limiting access to the God-created spiritual community of which we are a part. 'They', after all, are who we once were and in a sense still are: people to whom Jesus was first sent.

Thought questions

1. How can we be part of the community in which we live and worship, but stand up against the 'spirit of the age' that is so detrimental to human existence?
2. How might the language that is used to describe those who are not yet Christians be modified to be less likely to put up barriers?
3. How might the positive actions that Paul describes, 'extending hospitality to strangers' and 'weeping with those who weep', break down barriers and communicate a powerful message of what God's love is all about?
4. In what ways can we show that we follow God's leading by loving the world?

Dressing to Impress and Missional Thinking

The noted missionary, James Hudson Taylor, while working in China, was ambitiously attempting to spread the Gospel as quickly as possible. However, he and his team were struggling to reach out, or even physically get near, to locals in their houses. The solution Hudson Taylor arrived at involved sending single women out to meet the people, as these were seen to be less of a 'threat'. Most importantly, the women were clothed in traditional Chinese dress. And, in fact, Hudson Taylor saw fit to dress all of his team in traditional Chinese costumes. The positive effects of this move were seen immediately as the cultural barrier that was in place, primarily because of their European clothes, had been removed and the Gospel message was able to be delivered and people reached. What has a nineteenth-century missionary story to do with twenty-first-century Europe?

Hudson Taylor with his team in traditional Chinese attire.
Used with permission.

That Britain as a whole, like some other Western countries, has become a mission field is almost indisputable. No longer identifiably a Christian nation, the former Archbishop of Canterbury, Rowan Williams, was moved to famously characterise the UK as being a 'post-Christian country',[11] while others have used the less subtle term of 'pagan' to describe this fair land of ours.[12] Although not quite involved in the groundbreaking activity of Hudson Taylor in China, the stark reality is that, as things stand, Christians in Britain are essentially missionaries in their own country.

Such a missionary stance seems to come more naturally in other, more 'foreign', environments. Walking down Holloway Road on a morning just does not feel like a mission trip. So a missional attitude that involves being culturally engaging with the residents of the London Borough of Islington in the same way that Hudson Taylor was with the Chinese is not readily done. However, more and more, it seems that in order to reach out we need to be not only missional in our attitude, but missional in our thinking. This means breaking down cultural barriers so that the Gospel can be understood from within another's culture.

Being culturally aware is not an easy thing to do and requires godly wisdom and vision. For example, what could be more Christian than attending to an elderly patient's personal hygiene needs? There is the story of an imam being admitted to hospital due to chest pains and other complications. His condition deteriorated so he was transferred to an intensive care unit. Unusually, the nursing staff had some extra time on their hands one night, so decided to shave the patient's seemingly unkempt and unruly beard so that he would feel better once he woke up and realised he was clean-shaven. How proud the nurses were to have provided such personal attention to the man.

The feel-good factor was short-lived, however. One of the most important things about being an imam is that you are never supposed to shave. When the imam's family arrived and saw a clean-shaven father they were in shock. Culturally, this was not just a big no-no, but it was also inconceivable that this could have actually happened. As far as the imam's family was concerned, no beard meant no belief, and meant him being regarded as existing in a condemned state. The family left because it was inappropriate to look upon his

shaved face, and to go and make amends. Despite the nurses' seemingly good deed and intentions, the imam eventually died alone.[13]

Such incidents have led to a rise in the need for 'cultural competence' to be a key skill utilised in a wide range of professions: from business to education, health care to customer service. This is the expertise needed to work in cross-cultural situations, and includes understanding how gestures, clothing, practices and language – both verbal and body language – can impact on someone's ability to operate effectively.

This is not about compromise, but primarily about accessibility and acceptability. This can take into account all sorts of factors when dealing with people. One example might be time. It might seem reasonable for a doctor's surgery to be open from 9am to 4.30pm – with time off for lunch from noon to 1pm. However, if the local community is predominantly made up of hourly-paid workers, a big personal dilemma can arise. A person can be put into the position of choosing whether to receive pay or medical attention. Hence, a significant number of people are forced into deciding if seeking health care is more important than paying bills or even eating. Being culturally competent would mean being open at times when it is less likely that such a choice would be forced upon the people for whom you are trying to provide a service.[14]

That timing can be a cultural barrier is probably not something that even occurs to many of us. Sabbath school generally starts between 9.30 and 10am, and the main service anywhere from 11am to 11.30. Missionary thinking that encompasses cultural competence would force us to examine what might be regarded as a very straightforward and even neutral aspect of church. Is this the most culturally and chronologically accessible time for those in the community to whom we are trying to reach out . . . for those with families, for example? How might the distances that people need to drive to church affect the timing of the services we offer? How might the daily pattern of living in the community in which you worship affect programming?

Living in Britain means that this sort of analysis must happen more and more. The rich mix of cultures and ethnicities to be found across the country demands this. As John Storey notes, 'Britain has always been a hybrid nation,' and so one has never really been able to talk or write about British culture – because no such thing exists. Rather, we need to embrace the concept of there being not one, but many British cultures.[15]

Falling into the trap that this is just about culture being determined by ethnicity should also be avoided. There are all sorts of subcultures that emerge and then subside as the population ebbs and flows. From inner-city youth culture to farming communities in the wilds of Lincolnshire, from a Glaswegian to a Sotonian,[16] each have their own demands, peculiarities and even language – despite or in spite of the effects of globalisation. The barriers that need to be broken down by those reaching out to people in Brixton will be crucially different to the efforts required to reach out to folks in Bradford, Buntingford or Belfast . . . context is everything and changes everything.

Thought questions:
1. How might being a culturally competent church affect the behaviour of the church you belong to?
2. What are the different cultures that you interact with and

live among, and how should your church's behaviour vary because of them?

3. How can a community of believers become more aware of the culture and demands of the wider community in which they worship?

4. There are some very practical ways in which a church's context might itself be a barrier to reaching out – for example, where car parking is a challenge. How might such issues be addressed?

Dressing to impress: the unspoken barriers

So there we were, a couple of friends and I, playing golf in a beautiful setting on a beautiful day. The sky was blue and artfully dotted with perfectly white, fluffy clouds. The company was good and good-humoured. The quality of golf was patchy, but acceptable. Out of the corner of my eye, I noticed that an older gentleman was striding purposefully across a couple of fairways towards us. He did not have any golf clubs with him, which made it slightly incongruous behaviour given the setting. But as we moved forwards, he duly changed course and it became clear that he was intentionally on an intercept course with our group. His demeanour suggested that this was not going to be an amicable get-together; the set jaw and determined eyes spoke volubly to this.

Panicking, I tried to recall if I or anyone else had failed to replace a divot or repair a pitch mark, or had transgressed by failing to attend to one of the dozens of rules and regulations you need to try to remember as you navigate around a golf course. Attempting to be more positive, thoughts flitted in and out of my head along the lines that he had perhaps dropped something on his way around and so was merely on a search and rescue mission.

Eventually, he caught up with us. He was very polite, very old-school British and very insistent. It turned out that he was particularly passionate about scruffy golfers, and one of my fellow players and I had committed the heinous crime of failing to tuck our shirts into our trousers. Flappy shirt tails, even on a hot summer's day, were not acceptable on this particular course and in this particular club. We duly complied with his request and promised to carefully and faithfully study the guide in the clubhouse that outlined what was and was not acceptable attire so as to prevent any similar transgressions in the future.

I have yet to come across an Adventist church that has written its dress code down. A list of acceptable sartorial standards hanging up in the foyer as you enter a church building is, as yet, an unseen sight. But it is the unwritten rules that are also mostly left unspoken that are barrier making. To really be a part of Middletown Seventh-day Adventist Church, you see, you need to dress in a certain way, attain to certain standards . . . and that could be as much about dressing up as dressing down. This goes beyond what might be regarded as surface issues to embrace non-verbal messages, implications and insinuations. Despite being visitors, it was clear to us all that to be admitted into this golf club, you had to exhibit acceptable behaviour. The standard of behaviour required was clearly outlined. Joining the club meant that you had agreed to abide by the club's rules, which included tucking your shirt in and of course paying handsomely.

Thinking about a business setting briefly, research has shown that there are particular characteristics that people associate with the various dress codes to be found in that environment.[17] The familiar formal business suit and tie 'projects authoritativeness and competence', and the middling 'somewhat formal business attire' is linked to 'productivity and trustworthiness'. The more casual dress codes currently in vogue project 'creativity and friendliness'. Despite numbering myself among those who do not really care about fashion, one cannot deny that there is a link between what you wear and how you are perceived.

While carrying out the research into growing churches in Britain, a very noticeable aspect of the congregations, especially given my Adventist upbringing, was their 'dress code'. Out of nearly 5,000 people with whom I worshipped over the course of the research, fewer than 10 of the men were attired in suits and ties, and maybe double that number of women were 'dressed up'. It was clear that attending a church service in a British context does not now involve putting on your Sunday best. This phenomenon is cross-generational, cross-demographic and encompasses everyone from a street cleaner to a stockbroker.

As Viola and Barna point out, dressing up to attend a church service is a relatively recent phenomenon because only with the advent of the industrial revolution and mass-produced clothing in the late eighteenth century did the vast majority of the population even have an option of dressing up.[18] However, the concern here is to address the issue of dress from an accessibility point of view.

A neighbour of my local church told a fellow member that she much admired how smartly dressed our congregation was. As we streamed out from the church on a Sabbath morning, she thought we were all so well presented and seemed like such nice people. This and similar stories can be used as evidence that by behaving and dressing in the right way, we can witness positively to the communities in which our churches are located. However, the more important question to ask is whether that same neighbour felt compelled to don her best frock and hat and join us?

This discussion is partly related to the one on communication outlined above, because factors such as what we wear give out non-verbal messages. In fact, research suggests that non-verbal communication is vitally important because it is thought to be more sincere and honest than verbal communication.[19] The messages that our church service-attending attire gives out can be both negative and positive. If folks were flooding into our church services off the streets then fine. But if our attire hints at exclusivity then it becomes a barrier and a problem. If our neighbours see us all dressed up like we are going to a wedding every week, but only admire us from a distance as one might do those dining at a posh restaurant or top hotel . . . then again there might be an issue for us to think about. Likewise, a group of people who look like they have just wandered in off a building site might also be barrier building in certain contexts and certain places.

Someone related to me the story of how he invited several of his work colleagues to his baby's dedication. The colleagues duly turned up, and occupied one row in the centre of the church and near the front. They were dressed smartly, but casually smart . . . smartish. They were surrounded by a sea of other people, members, in suits and smart dresses and polished, gleaming shoes . . . the full kit and caboodle. Were his visitors made to feel unwelcome by what the church members said? No! Did they feel out of place and awkward because they were the only ones not dressed up like they were attending a marriage ceremony?

Well, who knows?

Part of the drive to dress up for church has to do with the idea that on Sabbath mornings we are going to meet God in the Lord's house. Dressing up to go and meet the Queen is a familiar and oft-used trump card here. However, as has already been established, the Lord's house is a spiritual one and God now dwells in people. Jesus will be among His people in a special way wherever they are gathered and however they are dressed. If churches start thinking about being accessible, then even the way we are dressed, whether going to church or not, might need evaluating: just as Hudson Taylor had to dress to impress, so we too might have to dress to impress the Gospel on people's hearts.

Thought questions

1. Should a church community be accepting of all people, no matter how they are dressed – and if so, how can a spirit of acceptance be encouraged?
2. How might you dress in your context to allow people to feel comfortable enough to attend a church service and listen to the Gospel message?
3. Thinking again about the example of Hudson Taylor, what other examples of culturally missional thinking might be applicable to where, when and how your church meets? For example – the timing of the services?

Practical Barriers

The story goes that two men who were camping out in the middle of nowhere set up their tent and settled down for the night. Several hours later, one of the men nudged the other and said, 'Look up and let me know what you see.'

'Wow, yeh,' comes the reply . . . 'I see countless stars.'

'Well what does that tell you?' asks the first man.

'It tells me that there are thousands, potentially millions of galaxies, it tells me that it is approximately 3.30 in the morning, it suggests that we are going to have a great day's weather tomorrow and finally it shows clearly the awesomeness of God and the vulnerability of man. What does it tell you?'

'It tells me that someone has stolen our tent.'

If you are not looking for it, you often will not see it. This is known as inattention blindness. Get people to concentrate on counting the number of passes made by a team of basketball players and they will often miss the bloke dressed up in a gorilla suit wandering slowly across the screen.[20] If you are not experiencing coming to your church's services as would a visitor, you will never see the very practical barriers that might be present and that actually discourage people from attending. Try 'going to church' as if you are a first-time visitor. Walk in their shoes, see things with new, critical eyes. Even better, get someone who has not attended church to visit and get their feedback. You may be surprised, both pleasantly and unpleasantly, at the outcome. To help in this process consider the following extra-long list of thought questions.

Thought questions

1. Are your church's parking spaces reserved for those who turn up early or for visitors from the local community?

2. If your place of worship does not have parking spaces, what other parking provisions could be put in place? Park and ride? Purchasing parking permits? Move?

3. What messages do the signs you have displayed in your church building communicate about you, your values

and aims? Are they more about what not to do than what to do: that is, don't eat, don't drink, don't talk, don't use a mobile phone, don't run, don't leave children on their own, and so on?

4. Are the toilet facilities clean, sufficient, well-signposted? Would you be comfortable to have them as the facilities on offer in your own home?

5. How are visitors welcomed? Are they greeted with an overwhelming hug that might be off-putting, laden down with MESSENGER magazines that mean nothing to them, made to alarmingly disclose their personal details straight away in a visitors' book or greeted appropriately and sensitively by someone who has the gift of greeting?

6. Is the building and its surroundings well-cared for, clean, well-maintained?

7. What does your building smell like? Musty? Dusty? Fresh?

8. Is the building warm when it is supposed to be warm and cool when it is supposed to be cool, or more like an igloo in the winter and a sauna in the summer?

9. Is your seating comfortable and accessible? Are the prime seats reserved with the judicious use of a hymnal or lesson book? How many of your seats have 'virtual' name plates on them? They might not have signs detailing whose seat it is, but we all know whose it is, right?

10. Are visitors offered a refreshing beverage or a scowl for chewing gum 'in church'?

Being Accessible: Inclusivity or Accommodation?

There is often a feeling that where the average restaurant is concerned, vegetarians are 'accommodated' rather than included. The majority of the menu is where the excitement is happening, where the effort is directed. Exotic flavours and combinations are tantalisingly described, in an attempt to lure spendthrift or unsuspecting customers into pricey selections. The vegetarian options, on the other hand, are just a necessary 'evil' that are rarely, if ever, the signature dish and are merely a way of catering for a small section of the population. 'Suitable for vegetarians' can at times scream out from the page that what is on offer is suitable in the sense that the dish is 'OK.' OK because there is no meat or meat products included and OK to eat; but what we vegetarians want is more than just OK . . . OK?

So yes, there were days of yore when having a vegetarian option that was not an omelette was rare – things have improved. But now, there is the impression at times, in some restaurants, that the wide variety of choice on offer makes it an exciting and mouth-watering occasion for most, whereas for the vegetarian it is a case of making do: ruminating over that head-spinning decision to choose between stuffed peppers or a feta and spinach lasagne. Are vegetarians and their cash welcome at such restaurants – of course they are? Do they feel included – well, maybe? Are they being accommodated . . . just.

One of the unseen barriers that might be erected in a church environment is the one that is put in place because of the effects of accommodating rather than including people. An example of this might be a visitor's Sabbath school class. At first glance, such an endeavour is well-meant and recognises that it is important to have Bible studies that provide access to those new to the profound riches to be found within the Bible's pages. The idea eventually being, of course, that once a visitor has mastered

the rudiments of the Bible, they may then advance to join the deeper, more sophisticated level of Bible study found in a Sabbath school class setting.

After all, there is all that in-house language to learn and be comprehended. Our favourite weighty theological terms, such as 'atonement', 'justification' and 'sanctification' can then be thrown around without fretting over whether they will be misunderstood . . . or even understood at all. Ellen White quotes can be rolled out without fear of alienation or ridicule, because her role in our church has been clearly explained. All the basic and elemental things have been covered and progression to the next level is permitted.

Those progressing from the visitor's class to a regular class must almost feel like donning a cap and gown. At long last they have graduated from the rudiments, the milk; and can now start to consume the meat, the heavy stuff. The issue to concern ourselves with here is the concept of 'them' and 'us', the move again from being outside to coming inside, from being a visitor to being 'normal' or even normalised. It may be that visitors' classes, or introductory Bible study groups, are necessary for a particular church's context. The important thing is to handle the language used, the unspoken implications, with sensitivity and understanding. To be seen to be inclusive, and not just accommodating.

Ideally, visitors would be brought into the general life of the church as quickly as possible. Ideally, studying the Bible would not be seen as a special task for people trained and steeped in the mysteries of its truths, but rather as a way of living and learning together. Ideally, the barriers that we put up unintentionally, and with good intentions sometimes, can be attended to. Ideally, we should not just accommodate those who are or appear different, but include them.

Thought questions:

1. How might the language that is employed in a church environment be excluding, accommodating or inclusive?

2. What other examples might there be of accommodating people rather than including them?

3. What barriers are we intentionally or unintentionally putting up to prevent those not yet in the church from entering?

4. How might we change the way we are, the way we behave, to enable as easy access as possible for those who are seeking out Jesus?

[1] As cited by Andrew T. Lincoln, *Ephesians* (Dallas, TX: Word, 1990), p. 141.

[2] Acts 21:28.

[3] He is called 'Trophimus the Ephesian' in Acts 21:29.

[4] Ephesians 2:15.

[5] Ephesians 2:16.

[6] Ellen Gould Harmon White, *Christ's Object Lessons* (Hagerstown, MD: Review and Herald Publishing Association, 1969), p. 386.

[7] This is its popular name and it should more correctly be called the American Express Centurion Card. Similar cards are available from other providers.

[8] Correct at the time of writing.

[9] Ellen G. White, *Sketches from the Life of Paul* (Washington, DC: Review and Herald Publishing Association, 1974), p. 42.

[10] E. G. White, 'How the Truth Should be Represented', *Review and Herald*, 25 November 1890.

[11] 'Former Archbishop of Canterbury: We Are a Post-Christian Nation' – *Telegraph, http://www.telegraph.co.uk/news/religion/10790495/Former-archbishop-of-Canterbury-We-are-a-post-Christian-nation.html* [accessed 21 October 2014].

[12] Lesslie Newbigin, *The Gospel in a Pluralist Society* (Grand Rapids, MI: Wm. B. Eerdmans Publishing, 1989), p. 213.

[13] Sourced from: Connie Sobon Sensor, 'Culturally Competent Care in the Workplace', *Imprint*, 53 (2006), 46–50.

[14] Lorin Cartwright and Rene Revis Shingles, *Cultural Competence in Sports Medicine* (Champaign, IL: Human Kinetics, 2010), p. 5.

[15] John Storey, 'Becoming British', in *The Cambridge Companion to Modern British Culture*, ed. by Michael Higgins, Clarissa Smith, and John Storey (Cambridge: Cambridge University Press, 2010), pp. 12–25 (p. 23).

[16] A resident of Southampton to you and me.

[17] Peter W. Cardon and Ephraim A. Okoro, 'Professional Characteristics Communicated By Formal Versus Casual Workplace Attire', *Business Communication Quarterly*, 72 (2009), 355-60.

[18] See Frank Viola, George Barna, *Pagan Christianity*, chapter 6, entitled 'Sunday Morning Costumes: Covering Up the Problem' for a more detailed discussion.

[19] See: Peter A. Andersen, *Nonverbal Communication: Forms and Functions* (Mountain View, California: Mayfield Publishing, 1999).

[20] Go to *http://www.theinvisiblegorilla.com/videos.html* to take the test!

SECTION 4

Being Engaging

Acommon caricature of a sales representative is that of a man with slicked-back hair who pushes his mid-ranged company car to the limit and to the detriment of other road users. He is, of course, a smooth talker with an unending stream of sales patter, and is the owner of a brain that is a repository of witty and convincing answers to all possible customer objections. His focus is on making the sale, driving through high-volume sales and winning that top commission.

He gives you, the customer or client, the nagging feeling that you are being manipulated into buying something you did not know you wanted and you do not actually need. The last you will see of such a salesman is the waving of the flaps on the back of his slick suit as he leaves you with a cloud of regret, an appliance you will use just once or an insurance policy of which you will never see the benefit.

In the world of sales this is known as a transactional approach. Where this style of selling is concerned, customers' actual needs are often just collateral damage in the pursuit of sales and the improvement of the 'bottom line'. It is thus the epitome of 'short-termism'. Relationships are transitory and incidental; and repeat sales are hardly ever achieved or even necessarily desirable. All the salesperson wants to do is to get you to buy – just the once. Their need to get to know you, the customer, is driven by their not-so-hidden agenda. They're not interested in what makes you tick, just what makes you buy. Whether you are a butcher, baker or candlestick-maker pales into insignificance compared to finding out whether you are the decision maker, and what clues you reveal as to what you might be scared or cajoled into buying.

A more enlightened style is known as the relational or relationship approach. Rather than seeing customers as a pool of punters of which to take advantage, the customer's perspective and needs are investigated and taken into account. It is a two-way, collaborative process that seeks to build a relationship of trust and mutuality. It sees a move away from sales patter to dialogue and information exchange, from short-term gain to long-term relationships, from it being all about benefiting the salesperson to an outcome where both buyer and seller gain.

You can spot such a salesperson because they might not even sell you something unless . . . wait for it . . . you actually need it. They will listen to what you have to say, without necessarily interrupting. They will metaphorically hold your hand and walk by your side, rather than handcuff themselves to you until you give in kicking and screaming.

One, hopefully, could never say that evangelists and evangelism are similarly manipulative, for by contrast people are regarded as being of prime importance. The underlying concern, after all, is that souls need saving. However, what about the methods employed? Unfortunately, the way we conduct evangelism often veers towards more of a transactional than a relational approach. All too often our system of belief – our Adventist doctrines – gets treated as if it were a product. Information delivery becomes the service being offered and so effort is channelled into ensuring that the ideas being put forward are presented in such a way as to prove they are correct and that all objections to them are overcome. The relational aspect can almost be secondary to what is deemed important . . . delivering that message.

An example of how transactional sales language and thinking is used, where evangelism is concerned, can be seen in the way that we often encourage others to make their 'decision'. So where a door-to-door salesperson is keen for Mrs Smith to make that all-important choice to buy a multi-functional vacuum cleaner, the evangelist's emphasis is on encouraging others to 'make a decision for Christ'. Just as a salesman is taught to look out for key signs or body language in order to understand when to force the sale through, so there are those who seek to use persuasion techniques that make use of psychological insights and an appreciation of body language to 'bring folks to Christ'.

Helping and encouraging potential Christians to come to a life-changing decision to submit to Christ is of course invaluable. However, there is perhaps reason to be prudently cautious before stepping over the line that results in evangelism becoming too sales-oriented, too slick;

moving from being encouraging and empowering, to pure manipulation. Beware of modern and postmodern citizens in general: they can readily detect a lack of authenticity, superficiality and that not-so-hidden agenda – 'sales, revenue and commission'.

There is, then, a tension between being professional about our evangelistic efforts and being too mechanical and business-like about them. For example, although often based on the parable of the sower found in Matthew 13:1-9, the evangelism cycle that is derived from this and similar passages is often disturbingly similar to a sales cycle. See, for instance, the examples given in figure 6.

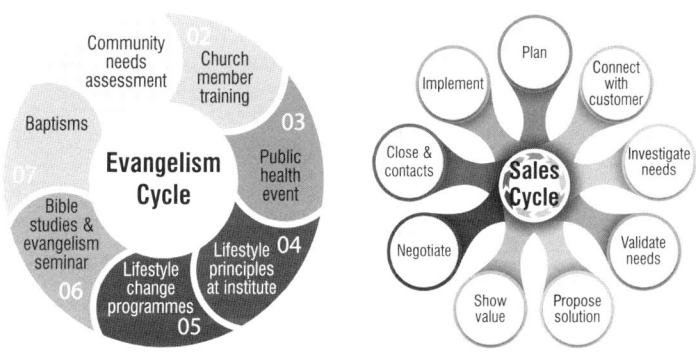

Fig. 6: *Evangelism versus Sales Cycle*

The parallels are self-evident. In both cases there is an assessment of needs, not with a view to offering 'acts of disinterested kindness',[1] but with a view to eventually 'closing the deal'. Where evangelism is concerned, value is demonstrated through the use of health and lifestyle

initiatives, the negotiation process and close are dealt with during seminars or crusades, and the implementation is arrived at through baptisms.

While we can obviously learn from other disciplines and apply them to our own situations, there is a danger that we forget that, at its heart, this is a spiritual undertaking. There might arguably be elements of transaction taking place when you become a Christian, but at its centre it must be all about relationships . . . because it *is* all about relationships.

Thought questions:
1. Do the evangelistic activities that take place in your church veer towards a transactional or a relational model?
2. Are there occasions when a transactional approach is actually a positive one? If so, why?
3. How might transactional evangelistic methods be appropriately combined with a relational approach?
4. For the people you know and are trying to reach out to, which approach do you think would work the best?
5. Some people appear to have the gift of being able to sell anything to anyone; how can that gift best be used in the building up of a church?

Being Three-dimensional: Part I

Being told you are one-dimensional is not usually a good thing. Former Australian prime minister Julia Gillard has had to withstand a whole shower of insults from rivals. One particularly notable barb sent her way by a fellow politician was the accusation that she was one-dimensional because she chose not to be a parent and so couldn't possibly understand them. Whether you are described as having a one-dimensional personality or being one-dimensional in your interests, it simply suggests that you are a flat, unimaginative person. It portrays you as a person who has a narrow and suffocating range of interests; it is a slur that suggests that you are ultimately boring and limited.

Evangelistic endeavours that are transactional in essence, and all about 'selling' ideas, beliefs and doctrine only, can end up being similarly one-dimensional and, if not 'boring' as such, then certainly limited. Pedrito Maynard-Reid, agreeing with this conclusion, suggests: 'Evangelism has traditionally been defined as the *verbal* proclamation of the good news of salvation.' He goes on to propose that a biblically-based evangelism model is a multi-dimensional one, and so involves both proclamation and demonstration.[2] As with a vacuum cleaner salesperson who is trying to convince you that his product will make your carpet look new, there is a need to *show*, as well as *declare*.

Both of the case study churches have a strong emphasis on *demonstrating* as well as *talking about* the Gospel. For example, Christchurch suggest that they 'wouldn't be happy just to send a street preacher out or only do the Alpha course, but actually we want to do things for the common good . . . for the betterment of society.'

It is also the case that Christchurch understand that Gospel proclamation is about:

'. . . believing that God is actually concerned with the plight of the poor, and wants to see us clothe the naked, feed the hungry . . . and that's actually a really big call on our lives.'

In Christchurch's case this includes being involved in the local foodbank, refugee mentoring, community football projects and helping improve the local environment by doing up a community garden.

Similarly, Kingsgate, in referring to missionary activities at home and abroad, suggested that it's all about ensuring: 'The Gospel is proclaimed in helpful ways and into the local communities. We have mission teams which go out to Africa and India, predominantly proclaiming the Gospel, but it's also proclaiming the Gospel, not in word alone, but in deed. So we have a whole social action department who are communicating the Gospel in the practicalities of people's lives.'

As with Christchurch, Kingsgate are involved in operating their local foodbank, an enterprise that is in fact the largest foodbank in the UK and one that helped 4,000 people in 2013. Kingsgate go that extra mile, so do not just supply food, but also have something called the Care Zone, a warehousing facility that stores supplies of '. . . good quality furniture, clothing, toys and household items – donated by church members and others in the community – that are given away free of charge to those that are in need in and around Peterborough.'[3]

Interestingly, Kingsgate also include one of their most successful initiatives as being about the 'proclamation of the Gospel'. A parent and toddlers' group called 'Mini Movers' provides a free service to the community and has resulted in eight people who were not previously Christians giving their lives to Jesus. Initially, this was not about providing a detailed explanation of the atonement or justification by faith, but an exhibition of neighbourly love.

However, the discussion on the nature of the Church, churches and their mission adds a further dimension . . . namely, engagement. For if God's mission, as realised in His Church, is grounded on spiritual communities, then a relational dimension is of paramount importance. For God's mission cannot be just about information transfer, but the building up of God-created spiritual communities and the reconciliation and unity that they represent. There is an inevitability that it must therefore involve relating to others.

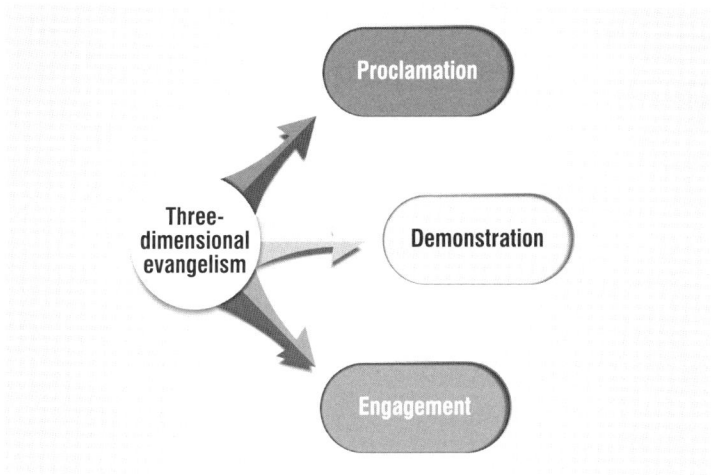

Christianity is about individuals . . . but not in isolation. If God dwells in people on three levels, then to be a Christian is in turn to be God's dwelling place on those same three levels. So yes, on an individual basis, that involves undergoing conversion, which results in God's Spirit dwelling in one's heart. But when taking into account the local and global elements that are part of what it means to be a Christian, we realise that this is not a solo undertaking – but a community-based one.

Hence, evangelism cannot just be about convincing someone of the need to believe, but must also include encouraging and enabling them to enter into the spiritual community that is to be found within a local church. This

does not mean that they as individuals disappear into a homogenous mass or that their distinctiveness is lost, but rather, this process entails God restoring them, thereby enhancing their individuality.[4] To proclamation and demonstration must therefore be added integration. The relational element cannot be ignored or downplayed. For we are not just saying, 'Believe what we believe,' but also, 'Come and be with us, come and be one of us, come and be part of us.' Thus there is a need for a church to be engaging in the sense that it promotes relationships through reciprocal connection.

Paul helps us to understand the countercultural and radical nature of what is going on here by referring to a 'new humanity', in Ephesians 2:15. This is the group of people who are at peace and reconciled to God and each other because of what God has achieved through His Son on the cross (see also Ephesians 2:16 here). It is evident that Paul has a relational approach in mind because of the journey that needs to be undertaken, which is to move from a state of separation to one of unity. This move is described as one in which those who are estranged, the so-called 'aliens' and 'strangers' (Ephesians 2:12), are brought together to become the 'citizens' and 'members of the household of God' (Ephesians 2:19). As a leading commentator on Ephesians suggests, the imagery that Paul uses in the book entails affinity and rapport.

'All this implies intimacy. Those who belong to God's household are members of the house, not necessarily kinsfolk, but certainly not slaves; nor are they "guests – here to-day and away to-morrow" – well treated when present but forgotten when gone.'[5]

Thought questions

1. What are the practical implications for how your church might reach out to people if a relational approach is adopted?

2. As with many aspects of Christian living, it's about balance. How can it be ensured that the correct balance between proclamation, demonstration and engagement is maintained in your church?

3. What are the practical ways a church might promote relationships?

Being Three-dimensional: Part II

Exploring the idea of engagement a bit further, Paul in Ephesians writes about engagement itself as being multidimensional. Reaching out, as just discussed, is itself a dimension of engagement. However, Paul reminds us about two further dimensions when it comes to engagement. Firstly, it is about reaching up. Remembering that the Church is all about Jesus, it naturally follows that if that is the case, then being part of the Church must involve a relationship with Him.

Additionally, the key role that the Holy Spirit plays in sustaining and empowering the Church inevitably means that a relationship with the Spirit is necessary. That the Church is created by God for His mission inevitably means that a relationship with God is necessary. None of this is groundbreaking in concept, but how about in practice? What does it actually mean to experientially and practically embrace the logical conclusions to these assertions? How can the Trinitarian understanding of the Church being described here lead us to reach up to God in three persons?

Paul addresses all of this beautifully in one of the prayers that are to be found in Ephesians, where in 3:16-19 he writes: 'I pray that, according to the riches of his glory, he may grant that you may be strengthened in your inner being with power through his *Spirit*, and that *Christ* may dwell in your hearts through faith, as you are being rooted and grounded in love. I pray that you may have the power to comprehend, with all the saints, what is the breadth and length and height and depth, and to know the love of Christ that surpasses knowledge, so that you may be filled with all the fullness of God.'

To relate to God in all three persons is to know God in all three persons. Strengthened by the Spirit, grounded in love in Christ, to be filled with the fullness of God . . . reaching up, for Paul, is a life-transforming, life-fulfilling, life-enhancing experience. Being an engaging church that reaches up is intimately related to being an accessible church: hence why some of these ideas are being repeated. For engagement is about giving those who are part of your church and those who are not yet part of your church opportunities to access God through your church; to provide access to that transforming, fulfilling and life-enhancing power that comes from relating to God in His fullness.

As far as the two case-study churches are concerned, allowing others to have access to God in His fullness has three additional, foundational elements: namely, word, worship and study – everything else is built on these. Biblical preaching is a key way of enabling people to access the word. Christchurch members describe this process from their point of view by saying: 'We're deliberately trying to even put our sermons on a level that will attract non-Christians into the auditorium as well. . . . it's trying to be careful with language, not using too much jargon, so just making it a bit more accessible, so not in any way watering down the truth we're proclaiming, but just talking about it in an accessible and relevant way for time and place, contextualising it for where we are.'

Where Kingsgate members are concerned, making the word accessible means enabling people to engage with it. This involves allowing a connection to be made between what the people hear preached and the way in which it can be relevant and applied to their lives. This starts, for them, with the preaching of the word on a Sunday. 'So, if you came here on a Sunday, [of] an hour-and-a-half-long service, probably 40 minutes of that would be a presentation of the word. We try to present it in a life-giving way so that it's actually got life application sewn into it. It's never dry and arid. It's our work as preachers to study the word and make it applicable . . . communicate it. Not just make it applicable, but communicate it in an applicable way.'

Kingsgate members then encourage each other and the attendees to personalise this through their small groups, or, as they call them, life groups, such that: 'It's applied because in every life group, a significant component of what they do on a Wednesday evening is to go through [the] word, and work through the individual application of it. You know we call for application on a Sunday, . . . we speak to 900 people, and we ask people to respond every week . . . and people do. But it's one thing responding in a group of 900 to the word, it's another when you are in a group of 10, and it's applied into the situations you're in, and your workplace and all that kind of stuff. So we've got a very high focus on the word and its application. It's the root of everything we do. . . .'

For Kingsgate, preaching well means delivering sermons that are 'intellectually stimulating', have 'biblical integrity',

and are presented in a 'life-giving way'. To the preaching of the word and study of the word in an accessible and engaging manner is further added worship.

'We do believe that there is something helpful, and encouraging, and building for people to invite their friends and colleagues, and all the rest, their family, to come into church, into . . . the presence of God in worship.'

Part of Christchurch's mission is for their church to be 'a vibrant spiritual community', such that they are able to: '. . . provide a context of engaging worship that helps people connect with God and learn to live well today.'

Different churches will approach this issue from different angles because of their diverse contexts. It is not one-size-fits-all, but through understanding the people you are reaching out to, it's a case of adapting and providing access through worship, word, study and a multitude of other ways. To those who are struggling to read, it might mean using more of a visual approach. For those who are expressive, it might mean a vibrant and invigorating worship time. For those who find meaning in formality, a more reflective and studied approach would appropriately be adopted. As my grandfather used to say, 'It's horses for courses.'

Thought questions:

1. We baptise in the name of the Father, Son and Spirit. How might we encourage others also to engage with all three through worship, study and the preaching of the word?
2. Thinking again about breaking down barriers, how might the way we are and do church allow for others to have greater access to God?
3. One of the key aspects of the case-study churches' approach is to preach with biblical integrity. How can we

ensure that the sermons we preach have that same integrity?

4. How can we ensure that we give the maximum opportunity for God to reveal Himself to others through word and worship?

5. Rather than word, worship and study, others have suggested word, mission and Spirit as a way of thinking about church. Which three terms would you choose and why?

Being Community: Part I

Mother Teresa is quoted as having said the following: 'The biggest disease today is not leprosy or cancer or tuberculosis, but rather the feeling of being unwanted, uncared for and deserted by everybody.'

Research into the effects of loneliness on health has backed up this assertion by providing a multitude of benefits which can be derived from maintaining human contact: including the ability to recover from periods of adversity to increased immunity.[6] However, loneliness is one of twenty-first-century Britain's biggest issues. The increase in the problem of loneliness has been linked by other research to a society that has become radically individualistic.[7] It is all about 'me, me, me' with barely a hint of 'we' or 'us'. Superficial solutions, such as the instant fame that comes with appearances on reality shows or talent contests, are desperately fought for. This is despite the many celebrities who have 'made' it, such as Beyoncé, who talk of their experience of isolation and loneliness.[8] However flawed the Localism Bill and the Conservative Party's push towards the Big Society might or might not be, these initiatives at least recognise that, as well as individuals, there is a need

to empower, improve and build up local communities.

There is a danger that if we do not engage with others when we reach out to them, then we are encouraging society's plummet towards greater and greater individualism . . . which is not part of God's plan for His Church, churches or humanity as a whole. To unashamedly repeat and remind, the role of the church in God's plan is to be a spiritual community and to encourage the growth of spiritual communities. This means that the purpose of evangelism or church growth initiatives is to do more than just generate, in union with God, individual Seventh-day Adventists. At its core, our evangelistic endeavours must include the aim to help God's mission to develop, encourage and cultivate Seventh-day Adventist communities.

In other words, it can never be enough for us to be satisfied by seeing an individual consent to Adventist beliefs and doctrine. Yes, we want folks to join our denomination and believe as we do, but primarily they are connecting to a God-created unity that is a spiritual community at a local and global level. Relational evangelism or friendship evangelism cannot just therefore be regarded as an option or a method, but as a life-saving, life-enhancing imperative.

One of the problems with adopting a transactional approach is that its lack of focus on the relational aspect of church rather soberingly places people in a vulnerable situation. Believing as we believe, and thinking as we think, does not mean that someone will automatically be part of us. Perhaps one of the most telling ways in which the tendency for our church to produce Adventists (individual) rather than Adventists (communities) is seen, is in what has become known as the 'back door problem'.

More than one in three people who join the Adventist

Church leave quietly, unobtrusively and, in many cases, unseen.[9] Now, migration out of the church is unfortunately always going to happen and for many reasons. However, it is not too much of a stretch to see that *part* of the problem is to be found in the way in which individuals come in through the 'front door', then remain as individuals, before eventually popping out of the back door. Entering as an individual means there is no connection with the community as a whole. Such people hang around in the household of faith, but are never part of what is going on. Enter as an individual, and then you are more likely to go out through the 'back door' as an individual.

Kingsgate have a highly proficient and professional set-up with a strong focus on connecting to people; however, this is not a cold, at-a-distance undertaking. Rather, they encourage the inviter to be part of the connecting process. So if a member of the church has brought along a friend, the church as an organisation does not then say, 'Well now, we'll take over and help connect that person to the church.'

But rather, it's the case that: ' "Bob's come with you" – right, so help them connect, and do that where there's already a relationship and already something that's working and healthy.'

In other words, engagement or connecting a person is done through the existing network of relationships that are already in place. With their invitational emphasis embedded into their cultural DNA, this comes very naturally to them. One of the hardest parts of being a church has already started to emerge and form . . . relationships.

Here then is an element of the second aspect of multidimensional engagement known as reaching in, or, in other words, being community. This is where a network of horizontal relationships and connections are nurtured. Paul, in Ephesians, gives us a number of ways that we can achieve this in chapter 4: '. . . speak the truth to our neighbours' (vs. 25), 'do not let the sun go down on your anger' (vs. 26), 'labor and work honestly', and 'share with the needy' (vs. 28), and 'let no evil talk come out of your mouths' (vs. 29).

This last command hints at a key element of community: namely, communication. Peter Ward, in his thought-provoking book *Liquid Church*, suggests that a modern-day incarnation of church should replace 'congregation with communication'.[10] Although that is a somewhat extreme suggestion, it makes the point that being community means talking to one another, socialising with one another, being with one another. In twenty-first-century Britain this is easier than it has ever been, with a multitude of social networking options through to cheap texting. There are resources available to have a constant flow of communication going on. It is the opportunity to move away from thinking about church just being those occasions when the saints gather on a Sabbath morning, to understanding that being church and a spiritual community has a wider meaning. This is not, however, a case for downplaying the most effective way to reach in: namely, face-to-face interaction. Despite the upsurge in social media and the opportunities it provides to connect, it ironically does not solve the problem of loneliness referred to previously. There is even a new term for the isolation that can still be felt in this age of social media – 'superconnected loneliness'.[11]

Thought questions:

1. How might the idea that church is about forming a network of relationships help influence the way that you

and your church reach out to people?

2. How can we make sure that the relationships that we are seeking to form with others are not superficial?

3. Not everyone who comes into a church's sphere of influence will already know someone. So how can their relational needs be addressed?

Being Community: Part II

If you want to win an election, one simple step is to use 'we' and 'us' in your speech more than 'I' and 'me'. Whether addressing the adoring hordes at the party conference or the floating voter in a marginal constituency, inclusive language is apparently the way to go. Research into the use of the individual and collective pronouns in campaign speeches shows that the winners greatly favoured inclusive rather than exclusive, egocentric language when compared to the unsuccessful candidates.[12]

There is nothing more galling than having pulled a proverbial all-nighter and brilliantly arrived at an innovative solution to a crisis situation, only to hear your boss claim the credit by telling all and sundry the things 'he' has done, rather than the things 'we' have achieved to put things right. Even the more inclusive 'my team' does not quite cut the mustard, because although statements such as, 'My team has increased sales by 150%' might appear to share the glory equitably, everyone knows whose team it is, and so the identity of the person who is really seeking the acclaim in this situation.

Inclusive talk, or 'us' and 'we' language, should be the language of choice for a church. There might be no 'I' in 'team', but there is also no 'I', in many ways, in 'church'. Paul's metaphors for the Church, which were referred to earlier – the body of Christ and the temple that is God's dwelling place – are all collective metaphors. Even the word 'church' is best understood as being a collective noun. It can therefore be understood that being a community means acting as a community, thinking as a community and speaking as a community. If the church is a God-created spiritual community taking part in God's mission, then it's not just you and me as individuals who are on this journey, but you and me together.

Now, of course there are lots of 'I's that go towards making up the 'we's, and we all have individual responsibilities and duties. The community context of the church and the individuals' contribution to that community are covered by Paul in Ephesians 4:11-13, where he writes: 'The gifts he gave were that some would be apostles, some prophets, some evangelists, some pastors and teachers, to equip the saints for the work of ministry, for building up the body of Christ, until all of us come to the unity of the faith and of the knowledge of the Son of God, to maturity, to the measure of the full stature of Christ.'

Here, Paul reveals the collective nature of the gifts of the Spirit, and particularly the leadership gifts. He is telling us that they are for ministry, for the building up of the Church, to enable spiritual growth among the body's members to happen. Although it is about individuals, the context is always community. 'I' may have been given the gift, but it is 'we' who are the intended beneficiaries.

This is very revealing in terms of the nature of what it is as an individual to 'be church', and has a number of everyday implications. As Adventists, we belong to a worldwide church that has fantastic healthcare and educational institutions, and an aid organisation, ADRA, of which we can be rightly proud. These shining stars of our denomination undoubtedly bring a sense of identity and purpose to it. There is also a rich repository of resources to be found online. Adventist sermons delivered by talented Adventist preachers that suit every taste are a mere click away. Although less so in isolated areas of the country, there are often churches aplenty to go and visit. The temptation to flit from one location to another is immense; a little pew surfing can be refreshing and revitalising.

These aspects of Adventism can direct our focus, energy and loyalty elsewhere. One of the things that we have to personally consider is, 'Have I got the balance right between being a member of a denomination and the member of a local church?' Thinking community, therefore, might also require refocusing our efforts, our loyalty and ourselves, locally: for the most tangible way of experiencing a God-created spiritual unity is to do so at the local level. As Stephen Miller eloquently puts it: 'Lasting legacy is birthed locally. It happens as fathers pour into their children, husbands pour into their wives, and pastors pour into their churches. We are made to be local people. To live in community. To know and be known.'[13]

When discussing our church's focus, it was suggested that we can easily, and even naturally, drift towards primarily having an inward focus. Therefore, we who are Adventists, as with any individuals who are members of a denomination, have an additional temptation of which to be aware: the tendency to have our focus drift away from the local to be dominated by or replaced with a denominational view. Yes, we gain a sense of identity and mission from denominational Adventism, but the local Adventist congregation, as with all churches, is where it is at.

There is a modern phenomenon that should also be mentioned here, one that further threatens our ability to focus locally: namely, being commuter churches. In some, but certainly not all, cases this is forced upon individuals because of their geographical locations. Whatever the circumstances, the identification with the local spiritual community is restricted and the connection we have with the community in which the church building is located is hampered to say the least.

Informatively, both our case studies, Christchurch and Kingsgate, are commuter churches. The way in which they address the need for a local focus is through their small-group structure. As discussed previously, both churches encourage a multi-dimensional approach in their small groups, all of reaching up, in and out. This type of small group has been described as a 'church in microcosm'.[14] It is a full expression of what it is to 'be church' and is one that being geographically based can provide a greater sense of 'localness'. The wider church still commutes to gather together; however, a focus on where people are is still able to be fostered and maintained.

A final consideration here is a less heavy, but much more practical one. The majority of the time, teams work better, are more efficient, and are less energy-draining than those individuals who attempt to go it alone. Yes, each individual has their thing to do, but as Michael Moynaugh suggests: 'There is a huge difference between a collection of individuals competing on a football pitch and a team. Christians are more likely to make a difference to the world if they act in teams than if they act alone.'[15]

Focusing locally means that one maximises the opportunity to benefit from others. However, being church brings with it more than just a group of people working towards a common goal. There is that relational element again, which means, where the church is concerned, 'team' also means 'family'. At times in church this seems to be more of a metaphor than reality! But it is telling that when Paul spends so much of his time writing about the nature of the Church in Ephesians, he uses the language of family. In Ephesians 2:19 he refers to the way in which all Christians are 'members of the household of God'. Society at the time was held together by the concept of the household, the wider family that all lived together and included everyone from slaves to master. All were part of the household and so all were family. Therefore, when Paul uses the word 'household' it is a term loaded with meaning and significance for his readers. It was the primary social unit at the time, and one that provided stability and structure.[16] So Paul using this as an image of what the Church is all about demonstrates the closeness and importance of spiritual communities as a household or family.

Such is the coherence between family, team and Church that Paul not only sees lessons to be learnt in terms of understanding the close-knit nature of the Church through understanding the nature of the household or family. He, in fact, applies a bit of reverse thinking in suggesting that the relationship between Christ and the Church is a model for the marriage relationship (Ephesians 5:21-33). As is often noted, there is no 'I' in team, and neither in the same sense is there in 'church'. But if you look closely into what the Church is all about, you can see that there is family, there is unity, and there is real community.

Thought questions:

1. Do you think your church is more a collection of individuals rather than a team? If so, what can be done to change that situation?
2. Churches are spiritual communities, as is often repeated in this book. How might the biblical view of church encourage teamwork?
3. What do you believe is the right balance between our membership of a denomination and of a local church?
4. How can we help ourselves and others understand the nature of what the Church should be all about, in terms of being a family in a society where the family unit is fracturing and diminishing?

[1]Here quoting Ellen Gould Harmon White, *The Ministry of Healing* (Nampa, ID: Pacific Press Publishing Association, 1942), p. 145.

[2]Pedrito U. Maynard-Reid, 'Holistic Evangelism', *Ministry* magazine, 73 (2000), 20-22 (p. 20).

[3]For more information see: *http://kingsgateuk.com/Groups/249919/KingsGate_Community_Church/Website/Peterborough/Community_Impact/Care_Zone/Care_Zone.aspx.*

[4]In referring to this aspect of church, Ellen White wrote: 'The perfection of the church depends not on each member being fashioned exactly alike. God calls for each one to take his proper place, to stand in his lot, to do his appointed work according to the ability which has been given him.' Ellen G. White, *Manuscript Releases*, vol. 21, nos. 1501-1598, Letter 19, 1901, pp. 277, 278.

[5]Ernest Best, *Ephesians: A Shorter Commentary* (Edinburgh, New York: A&C Black, 2003), p. 117.

[6]John T. Cacioppo, 'Rewarding Social Connections Promote Successful Ageing' (presented at the AAAS Annual Meeting, Hyatt Regency, Chicago, 2014).

[7]Jo Griffin, *The Lonely Society* (Mental Health Foundation, 2010).

[8]Beyoncé, discussing her feelings of isolation, says: 'I guess I was a bit lonely and I wanted to talk to someone so I opened up my computer and I just talked.' From her DVD: *I Am . . . World Tour* (RCA, 2010).

[9]For further information see *http://www.adventistarchives.org/welcome.pdf.*

[10]Pete Ward, *Liquid Church* (Massachusetts: Hendrickson Publishers, 2002), p. 120.

[11]Stephen Marche, 'Is Facebook Making Us Lonely?' in *The Best American Science and Nature Writing 2013*, ed. by Siddhartha Mukherjee and Tim Folger (Boston, MA: Houghton Mifflin Harcourt, 2013), pp. 288–301 (p. 290).

[12]'Power through "Us": Leaders' Use of We-referencing Language Predicts Election Victory', Niklas K. Steffens, S. Alexander Haslam, 2013.

[13]*http://www.worshipcohort.org/beauty-local-church/.*

[14]Graham Cray, *Mission-shaped Church: Church Planting and Fresh Expressions of Church in a Changing Context* (London: Church House Publishing, 2004), p. 53.

[15]Michael Moynaugh, *Being Church, Doing Life: Creating Gospel Communities Where Life Happens* (Oxford: Monarch Books, 2014), p. 40.

[16]For the big influence the concept of the household has on the New Testament see: Carolyn Osiek and David L. Balch, *Families in the New Testament World: Households and House Churches* (Louisville, KY: Westminster John Knox Press, 1997).

Being Church - Contextually

When I was growing up, my cricketing idol was Graham Gooch: a man who still holds the record for the most test runs scored by an Englishman. Now, there are two things that distinguish competent or even very good cricketers from great cricketers. Firstly, the very best batsmen seem to have more time than anyone else. For mere cricketing mortals, like the majority of us, watching a ball being hurled towards us at over 90mph would not only be terrifying but over before we could even nervously twitch, let alone respond with any intention. Elite batsmen seem to almost have time to sip a cup of tea before nonchalantly dispatching the ball to the boundary. Secondly, when they hit the ball, the sound of leather on willow is distinctive. It's not just that they hit the ball hard, but there is a reverberation, an aural solidity, a definitive crack that makes everyone around the ground sit up and take notice. When Goochie was batting at his best, he was a man who seemed to have that extra time at the crease . . . in both senses of the phrase. His batting was accompanied by a resounding, attention-grabbing noise each time his blade came into contact with the ball.

Being an impressionable young lad, I decided that to maximise my potential as a batsman, I needed to bat just like Graham Gooch. I didn't grow his distinctive Zapata moustache – mostly because facial hair at the time was not an option for me. I couldn't afford one of his famous white helmets. His lumbering, somewhat morose demeanour was also not really for me . . . maybe not consciously anyway. However, the way he stood at the crease and the innovative manner in which he lifted his bat up before the bowler delivered the ball were adopted with enthusiasm and hope. I was not alone in doing this; a slew of amateur and professional cricketers around the country at the time adopted this expectantly sure-fire method.

An undistinguished cricketing career at various schools duly followed. To date I have scored exactly the same amount of runs as the Queen has for our country. At no stage did I ever have the time at the crease to play my shots like Graham Gooch, nor did the occasional man and his dog walking around the boundary remotely take notice because of the sound of my bat meeting the ball. It did not take long to realise that merely copying how someone does things does not mean that you will experience the same success they have.

It is extremely tempting also to copy other successful methods or models for church growth. As mentioned in the introduction, our church has, with good intentions, copied among others both Willow Creek and Saddleback; Adventist evangelism models developed in North America and other places have been seized upon with relish. The propensity to copy others is seen in the envious glances thrown towards evangelistic work being done by Adventists in South America, or the innovative Happy Hands project in Copenhagen, Denmark. The thinking goes that if the same programmes, literature or style of speaker are used in a new location, then the same uplifting results will be experienced again . . . be they multiple baptisms, a spiritually enlivened congregation, increased attendance, and so on. Failure is often put down to poor execution. It is just a case of putting greater effort into exactly reproducing the model and replicating the methods.

Now, this is not to disregard the benefits of learning through modelling. Modelling others is an excellent way of learning through observation, listening and, above all, participation. However, importing wholesale another's methods into your context almost without exception does not work. This is because another's context is not your context. Their situation is not your situation. The people who make up their community are not the same people who make up your community. The people they want to and are able to reach out to are not the same as the ones with whom you are interacting. Hence, Kingsgate and Christchurch's stories can be used as sources of inspiration, as examples of how 'being church' is reflected in what a church does. But the enticement to merely copy should be resisted.

A key principle to take on board is that each of us is part of a unique spiritual community. We are all part of a particular cultural context in the UK and so are partaking in God's mission in a distinct, even specialised manner. It must be this way, because the people who make up your community and my community are different. The diverse locations in which we find ourselves and our irreplaceable combination of spiritual gifts means that each individual God-created spiritual community is uniquely positioned. Therefore, each spiritual community needs to adapt to its own situation while at the same time maintaining core values and beliefs. Every group of Christians necessarily needs to tailor its approach for the sake of bringing the Gospel in all its forms to those around them.

Although this is extremely challenging, Ellen White suggests that this is in fact Christ's method. She has famously written that to follow Christ's method is all about learning 'to adapt our labours to the condition of the people – to meet men where they are'.[1] Now, this is not just about meeting people where they are in terms of their location, be it the city, or village; the pub, the playground or the park. It is not just about getting people to leave the safe haven of the church and their homes, but is also about meeting people where they are in their own context.

In that same article, Ellen White notes how Paul did not reach out to non-Jews by 'exalting the law', but by 'exalting Christ'. On the other hand, he also reached out to the Jews by giving 'due honour to the ceremonial law'. Different people, different approaches, you see. If the ceremonial law had been emphasised in his approach to the Gentiles, then Paul would have come unstuck. Happily, he exhibited the ability to adapt what he did to the context he found himself in . . . so meeting the people where they were.

The need to show this same adaptability and flexibility can crop up in a multitude of situations. For example, Ellen White advocates this same approach with regard to diet. In

one particular situation she was addressing the issue of diet and those people who could not afford expensive health foods. 'There are poor families whose diet consists largely of bread and milk. They have little fruit and cannot afford to purchase the nut foods. In teaching health reform, as in all other gospel work, we are to meet the people where they are. Until we can teach them how to prepare health reform foods that are palatable, nourishing, and yet inexpensive, we are not at liberty to present the most advanced propositions regarding health reform diet.'[2]

Similarly, on another occasion, Ellen White tells the story of how her secretary Sara was called to minister to a family where all the members were sick. Again, one of the lessons that can be learnt is that different circumstances and different people require alternative approaches. 'The father belonged to a highly respectable family, but he had taken to drink, and his wife and children were in great want. At this time of sickness there was nothing in the house suitable to eat. And they refused to eat anything that we took them. They had been accustomed to having meat. We felt that something must be done. I said to Sara, Take chickens from my place, and prepare them some broth. So Sara treated them for their illness, and fed them with this broth. They soon recovered.

'Now this is the course we pursued. We did not say to the people, You must not eat meat. Although we did not use flesh foods ourselves, when we thought it essential for that family in their time of sickness, we gave them what we felt they needed. There are occasions when we must meet the people where they are.'[3]

A final example taken from Ellen White's writings concerns being flexible and contextual when it comes to the words used to communicate. She suggests that our instructions should 'not . . . be of a character to perplex the mind'.[4] Particularly she addresses the propensity for some to use complicated or what she calls 'lofty' language, writing: 'When feasting upon God's word, because of the precious light you gather therefrom, present it to others that they may feast with you. But let your communications be free and heartfelt. You can best meet the people where they are, rather than in seeking for lofty words which reach to the third heavens. The people are not there, but right here in this sorrowing, sinful, corrupt world, battling with the stern realities of life.'[5]

Meeting people where they are involves more than just meeting people where they are in terms of their location. It is not just an injunction to meet folks in their homes, workplaces and the local shopping malls. Meeting people where they are involves meeting them in their context . . . be it sociological, psychological, spiritual, intellectual or more. It's about where people are in their lives and on their life's journey. This introduces a complexity to evangelism that is often missing or difficult to account for: for each individual brings with them their own context, language and culture.

Thought questions:

1. Where are the people you are trying to reach out to in terms of their life's journey, their culture, their language, their spirituality, their social location?

2. How might you need to adapt the way you 'are church' in order to make your community as accessible as possible to them?

3. Perhaps one of the biggest factors is the age of the people

being reached out to. How can this aspect best be attended to?

Being Church: Valuing, Not Just Doing

I have been through a values-generating process for various groups and organisations a number of times. Often the problem is that this is a paperwork exercise that has no bearing on reality, and certainly does not reflect what is happening on the 'factory floor', or, in a church's case, up and down the aisles. The most famous example of the disconnect that can exist between stated values and values as seen in practice is that of Enron. One of their four key values was 'integrity', something that the 16 former Enron executives who received prison sentences for various questionable accounting practices obviously failed to embrace.

'Authenticity' can seem like a meaningless buzzword to some, because, as long as you are authentic, then it does not matter what you are being authentic about. You could be an authentically horrible person, and as long as you remain faithful to your horribleness then your authenticity is affirmed. Despite the apparently shallow nature of the term, what people are looking for is a connection between words and deeds. It's not enough to say you are a family person if you don't spend any time with your family. It's easy to say that you are an advocate of social justice, but to be convincing about that position you need to be on the case when injustice arises.

The challenge for churches is not just to state what values it would be nice to have, but to actually embed them into the church's culture, such that they become second nature, part of who the church is. We have come back full circle to the concept of being versus doing. Christopher J. Wright has put the issue succinctly by writing: 'To say "missional church" is like saying "female woman". If it isn't female, it isn't a woman; if it isn't missional, it isn't the church.'[6]

Being missional is one of the key values that we have looked at in this book, along with connecting with others through being accessible and engaging. As with being missional and doing mission, it is not enough to provide access or engagement. Churches that value the biblical concepts of accessibility and engagement are not churches that just provide access and partake in engaging activities. Rather, they are churches that are innately accessible and engaging. Just as my chance encounter with a chorister from the St John's College choir made it clear that here was not just someone who sings, but a singer, so with church; it should be our aim, with God's help, to be churches that do not just engage, but are engaging; that do not just give access, but are accessible; that do not merely do mission, but are missional.

The final words are Paul's final words to the Ephesians, found in Ephesians 6:23-24: 'Peace be to the whole community, and love with faith, from God the Father and the Lord Jesus Christ. Grace be with all who have an undying love for our Lord Jesus Christ.' Amen.

---

[1] E. G. White, 'How the Truth Should Be Represented', *Review and Herald*, 25 November 1890.
[2] Ellen Gould Harmon White, *Testimonies for the Church* (Nampa, ID: Pacific Press Publishing Association, 1948), vol. 7, p. 135.
[3] Ellen Gould Harmon White, *Counsels on Diet and Foods: A Compilation from the Writings of Ellen G. White* (Hagerstown, MD: Review and Herald Publishing Association, 1946), p. 466.
[4] Ellen Gould Harmon White, *Testimonies for the Church*, vol. 6, p. 58.
[5] Ellen Gould Harmon White, *Counsels to Writers and Editors* (Hagerstown, MD: Review and Herald Publishing Association, 1946), p. 87.
[6] Christopher Wright, quoting Birger Nygaard: Christopher J. H. Wright, 'The Whole Church Taking the Whole Gospel to the Whole World: The Vision of Lausanne' (presented at the Spring Lectureship, AGTS, 2010): *http://www.agts.edu/encounter/articles/2010summer/wright1.htm.*